"Vickie Stringer, author, founder and publisher of Triple Crown Publications, is the reigning queen of urban fiction."

- *Publisher's Weekly*

"Ms. Stringer has entered the slightly more rarefied precincts of book publishing. And she's getting rich."

- *The New York Times*

"After being rejected by 26 publishers, Vickie Stringer's self-published novel became a bestseller."

- *Entrepreneur Magazine*

"After a bit of research, Stringer started her own publishing company, Triple Crown Publications, and published Let That Be the Reason in 2001. In just three weeks, she sold 1,500 copies."

- *Black Issues Book Review*

In 2001, [Stringer] set up a small company, Triple Crown Publications, to publish [her] novel. Today Triple Crown publishes more than a dozen authors. The company sold 300,000 paperbacks during a recent 16-month period…"

- *The Washington Post*

"In less than two years, Triple Crown has established itself as the premier publisher of hip-hop fiction."

- *Columbus Monthly*

"Vickie Stringer has got an American Dream in her own hands."

- *Blast* Magazine, Japan

"[Stringer] has taken the company from a one-woman operation to nine full-time employees, with revenues approaching seven figures and a major deal with a foreign publisher."

- *Essence* Magazine

"Mainstream publishers wouldn't touch her book. So Stringer printed 1,500 copies and took to the road. The book became an underground hit, and bookstores began to stock it."

- *Newsweek*

Triple Crown Publications
2959 Stelzer Rd., Suite C
Columbus, Ohio 43219
www.TripleCrownPublications.com

Library of Congress Control Number: 2005933943
ISBN: 0-9767894-0-X
Cover Design/Graphics: Bob James & Evangelia Philippidis, Silver Moon Graphics
Author: Vickie M. Stringer with Mia McPherson
Associate Editor: Maxine Thompson
Editor-in-Chief: Mia McPherson
Consulting: Vickie M. Stringer
Hair, Make-up and Styling: Monecka Freeman
Photography: Peter Chin

First Trade Paperback Edition Printing October 2005
10 9 8 7 6 5 4 3 2 1

Printed in the United States of America

About the Authors

Queen of Hip-Hop Literature Vickie Stringer has revolutionized the literary industry as a pioneer of the Hip-Hop Literature genre. Beginning with the self-publishing of her first novel, the *Essence* Best Selling *Let That Be the Reason*, followed by the founding of her internationally renowned publishing company, Triple Crown Publications, Stringer's innovative voice and controversial style has earned her intrigue and fascination around the globe.

The successes and achievements of Stringer's novels, *Let That Be the Reason*, its sequel, *Imagine This*, the upcoming *Dirty Red*, and the wide popularity of the Triple Crown Publications brand have garnered attention from prominent news media since Stringer ignited the Hip-Hop Literature era less than four years ago. In addition to being featured in *The New York Times*, *Newsweek*, MTV News, *Publisher's Weekly*, *The Boston Globe*, *Vibe*, *Essence*, *Entrepreneur* and *Inc.* Magazine, in April of 2005 Stringer and Triple Crown Publications became international as her novels were translated and released in Tokyo, Japan.

In 2004, Stringer also founded The Valen Foundation, a non-profit organization named for her son, to reunite and restore bonds between children and their incarcerated parents.

***

Mia McPherson is the Editor-in-Chief at Triple Crown Publications. Mia is a native of Pittsburgh, Pennsylvania and holds a bachelor's degree in Journalism from The Ohio State University.

Dedication

This book is dedicated to those who dare to dream. There is a spot on the bookshelf waiting just for you!

And to My Son and Reason for Living, Valen. Thank you for sacrificing with Mom for the company. Thank you for understanding when we had to move to save money and when Mom has to work late.

Acknowledgements

First and always I'd like to acknowledge God and His mercy.

An extra special thanks to my co-author Mia McPherson for bringing a polishing rag to this project. It is an honor to work with you.

I want to acknowledge those who made my company a success. My lawyer, F. Robert Stein – without your guidance, there is no way that my company would have the foundation that you have insisted that I lay. When obstacles come up, you never judge me for my errors and for trusting and not getting things in writing. Instead, you appreciate my ethics and help me through the rough legal issues. I am forever grateful for your guidance.

To my authors, present and future, who have written best-sellers and gave my company a chance - T.N. Baker, Tracy Brown, Quentin Carter, Darrell DeBrew, Keisha Ervin, K'wan Foye, Trustice Gentles, Joylynn Jossel, Kane & Abel, Darrell King, Lisa Lennox, Victor Martin, Mallori McNeal, Jason Poole, A.J. Rivers, Danielle Santiago, Leo Sullivan, Nikki Turner, Tu-Shonda Whitaker, Kashabma Williams.
To Maxine Thompson for her editorial guidance.

To My Staff at Triple Crown Publications who believed in my dream and now share my vision. Without your hard work and sweat, we would not be where we are today. Tammy Fournier, Mia McPherson, Kaori Fujita, Aaron Johnson, Deidre Johnson, Benzo Stringer. Those before you, after you and to come.

To the distributors who pushed and pushed my products. African World Books, Nati, you have never paid an invoice late.

To the store managers who were open to giving a new book a chance. Black Arts Plus, George Miller, you were the first bookstore to stock my books.

An extra special thanks to Steven Berry for your creative direction and for my website, and who was with me in my living room, dreaming.
A special thanks to Keith of Marion Designs for my company's book covers.

An extra special thanks to Evangelia Philippidis who not only designed my first book cover for my own self-published book, *Let That Be the* Reason, but also this book cover to share with the world.

To Dan Poynter for your support.

To Malloy Printing and Tim Scarbrough for believing in my company and working so hard to allow me to reach my goals.

To Ron Cunningham, Judy and the entire Malloy Printing.

To Franklin White (*Fed Up With the Fanny, Cup of Love, Money For Good*), you encouraged me to do this thing called self-publishing. Thank you for always being there for me, and...I hope I have made you proud.

To UPS rep Lee Marshal who started me shipping with one book. Look at our volume now.

An extra extra extra extra special thanks to all of my readers, fans and supporters…without you, Triple Crown Publications would not exist.

To the media, ABC News, *Adlib Magazine, BMR Magazine,*

Black Enterprise Magazine, Black Issues Book Review, The Boston Globe, Blast Magazine, Call and Post, Can Cam Magazine, The Columbus Dispatch, Columbus Monthly, Complex Magazine, Don Diva, Entrepreneur Magazine, Essence Magazine, Inc. Magazine, King Magazine, Luire Magazine, MTV, *Murder Dog Magazine,* NBC4, *The New York Times, Newsweek Magazine, Nylon Magazine, Popeye Magazine, Publishers Weekly, Parle' Magazine,* Power 107.5, *The San Francisco Chronicle, Scwaii Magazine, Source Magazine, Tokyo Headline,* The Tom Joyner Morning Show, WOSU TV, *Vibe Magazine, The Washington Post, Woofin Magazine, Woofin Girl Magazine,* UPN, *Upscale Magazine.*

So many people make you a success. I could never list them all. But know that I thank you every chance I get and I will give a BIG Thank you to everyone.

For this, I am so grateful.

If your name is not listed…sign your name here

____

How to Succeed in the Publishing Game

Table of Contents

Disclaimer

How to Succeed in the Publishing Game is an instructional book intended to encourage and guide those who are considering entering the field of self-publishing. While this book provides valuable information and tips on how to succeed in self-publishing, it is by no means all-inclusive. This book may contain errors, and is only current to the publication date.

Throughout the book and in the book's Resource pages, you will find other recommended references and reading. Use these and other sources for further information. It is also strongly suggested that you seek legal advice throughout all stages of the self-publishing process. Utilize all of the information that you can find to help you to decide if self-publishing is right for you, and to determine how, and if, to self-publish.

Introduction

We celebrate a time where now, writers are being heard in record numbers. Never before in history have self-published authors received a greater welcome. Major publishing houses like Simon & Schuster, Random House and Harper Collins, just to name a few, are taking notice of over-looked talent. There are many trailblazers before us.

John Grisham, Terry McMillan, E. Lynn Harris and so many more have paved the way. From economics to just plain making dreams come true, self-publishing can be a vehicle for achieving the American Dream. It is time to roll up your sleeves and make it happen for yourself. No one can dream your dream but you. And only you can see your dream in color. Now make it a reality by doing the necessary work.

If I can do it, so can you. Come on…Let's read how!

My First Book Sale

The past four years of my life have been as overwhelmingly wonderful as they have been challenging. I guess the term "pleasure with pain" was meant for me. Although I have experienced an upward change in my income, my lifestyle and my opportunities—all of which came with great sacrifice—I have endured the loss of people whom I thought were my friends. Needless to say, this caused me some anguish. Even so, at the same time, I have gained responsibility for the lives and the careers of my literary agency clients, for which I am grateful. But, through it all, I wouldn't change anything for my journey.

For my very first sale, I approached a lady working in a hair salon. As she stood behind the chair, I held up my book and I asked her to buy it. I can remember her looking over the book without reaching for it. All the while my stomach was turning and my nerves were getting the best of me. The biggest fear with hand-to-hand selling is the fear of rejection. Anyhow, I stood there, took a deep breath and trusted that my novel was worth the ten bucks I was charging. Inwardly, I reassured myself that if she didn't buy, someone else would.

The lady's name was Leah.

"Do you like to read?" I asked, holding my book out for her to peruse.

She didn't take it right away, but then again, I didn't pull it back out of her face, either.

Finally, Leah relented. Grabbing my book, she looked at the glossy cover and her curiosity piqued.

"It's only ten dollars," I chimed.

"What's it about?" Leah asked.

"A Female Hustler."

Silence fell between us.

"You won't regret this buy." I smiled at her.

"Well..." She paused. Then, reluctantly, she dug into her jean pocket.

She pulled a ten dollar bill out of her pocket. I almost snatched it out of her hand, I was so excited.

I gave the book to her.

"You not gone sign it?" Leah asked.

Nervously, I signed the book, hands trembling.

"What's your name?"

"Leah."

> *To Leah,*
> *Please enjoy my first novel.*
> *Always ,*
> *Vickie Stringer*

I can remember walking out of the salon, feeling on top of the world. I had made my first book sale for ten dollars. Regardless of the successes that followed, I will never forget my first customer, my first sale, and my first signature. Just think. I had written something that the world was waiting for...
Dare to dream...

For several years, I can remember wanting to write a book. As time went by, the desire burned inside of me until it was all that I could think of. Even so, it was hard to tell people about what I was doing. No one understood or believed quite like I did.

Writing a book is a lifelong dream for so many. But there was no doubt in my mind. I knew that I had a story to tell. Once I wrote it, I had to find a way to sell it. So how did I accomplish this? Let's get down to business.

You Want to get Published

You've spent months, even years preparing, researching and writing your book. It's only logical that you now want your masterpiece to be seen by as many readers as you can possibly reach. How do you achieve this?

In previous years, the conventional way to get your book published was to solicit the major publishing houses. Simon & Schuster, Random House, St. Martin's Press and the other big name New York companies were the most desirable and most sought-after channels for publishing a book. Inasmuch as there are thousands upon thousands of new books written each year and so few major publishing houses, this option just isn't realistic for many authors.

Fortunately, in recent times, with the help of many technological advances, self-publishing has become a widely popular alternative to the major publishing houses. With today's ease of printing and the feasibility of having a book printed in a matter of weeks as opposed to months and years, more and more authors are reaping the benefits of becoming a self-publisher.

What is Self-Publishing?

Self-publishing means that you essentially create your own business wherein you are in charge of each step of the publishing process. Where with a major publishing company, an author would simply submit his or her manuscript to an editor and the company would take care of the production process, *you* are the company. You deal directly with the editors, typesetters, graphic designers, printers, media, distributors, etc. You handle your own marketing and publicity. You decide which distributors will carry your book. You handle your own finances, profits, royalties. You control the future of your work.

Other Publishing Options

The majors

Getting a book deal with one of the major publishing companies used to be the ideal situation for most authors. Many times, a large advance is involved, authors collect royalties and after completion of the manuscript, the work is turned into a book with little more effort made on the part of the author. However, with the rising popularity and success of self-publishers, more authors are benefiting from the increased control, higher profit and more effective marketing and promotion that goes along with successful self-publishing.

Vanity or subsidy publishers

Vanity publishing, also called subsidy publishing, is another available channel for publishing a book. Vanity publishers produce a book much like a major publishing company would—you supply the manuscript, they take care of the production aspects of publishing and even offer to promote and distribute your book. However, you as the author, must pay the vanity publisher to publish your book. Unlike negotiating a book deal with a large publishing company, you do not collect an advance or receive royalties. Unlike self-publishing, you will have little control in the production of your work. Vanity publishers make it possible for many authors who do not have the time to self-publish or may otherwise be overlooked by major publishers to see their work in print.

On the down side, though, most vanity publishers have alarmingly high failure rates, and bookstores are often reluctant to put books published by vanity publishers on their shelves. Because vanity publishers are out to make money, they will likely publish work without much regard for quality or content. As promotion and sales rates are often low, vanity publishing is an option, however risky.

ePublishing and eBooks

ePublishing, or electronic publishing, is a form of digital publishing wherein a book is viewed online rather than printed and bound in the standard book format. ePublishing can be another form of self-publishing, or an eBook may be sold to a pre-established ePublisher. Because of the growing popularity and ease of selling and marketing products on the Internet, eBooks have become increasingly accepted in the publishing world. Instead of physically printing your book, ePublishing makes it possible to package, distribute and sell your book, in the form of an electronic file, via the Internet. While eBooks are significantly less costly to package and distribute than a printed and bound book, many readers find it displeasing to read from a computer screen and prefer the ease of reading from conventional book pages.

The Advantages of Self-Publishing

As self-publishing becomes increasingly popular among authors who desire to have more freedom with their work, be more proactive in the production, publicity and marketing departments and seek to gain more profit than with a major company or vanity publisher, more authors are realizing the benefits of becoming a self-publisher.

You are an expert in your field of writing.

Whether you have written a fiction novel, a self-help book or an autobiography, you are essentially an expert in your field. You have done the research, and you have spent the time to perfect your knowledge in your subject of interest. Therefore, you are able to target your market directly. Many books published by major, mainstream publishers have failed because of the inability to target the market. The inability to target the correct audience leads to improper marketing, which leads to low sales and ultimately an unsuccessful book. Knowing and targeting your market is a key factor in successful marketing, and is a sure-fire way to increase the popularity and expand your readership.

You get to keep more money.

As a self-publisher, the profits of your book are yours. Brokering a deal with a major publishing company can often mean that an author will receive a large advance and a small percentage of each sale of the book. As a self-publisher, *you* are the company. You don't have to settle for a percentage of each sale, as each sale is yours and yours alone.

You can get your book on the market quicker.

With the advances in printing, and the vast number of existing printing companies, it is possible to print your book in a matter of weeks. You will not have to wait for the release of your book according to the schedule of a large publishing company. You can set your release date for whenever you choose. The faster you produce your book, the faster you can get your book out on the market. You don't have to worry about your information or subject matter becoming outdated before the book even reaches the shelves.

You control the rights and actions of your own work.

You don't have to worry about a large publishing company owning a percentage of your movie rights or television appearances.

If your book goes international, you don't have to worry about the portion of the translation rights going to another company. You can choose what to write, when to write it and can capitalize on all the benefits.

You can publish whatever you want without anyone's approval.

More often than not, authors are rejected by large publishing companies. It may be the content, the style or the subject matter that does not fit the image that a large publishing company is looking to achieve. As a self-publisher, you don't have to wait for the approval of another publishing company to reach your readers. You believe in your work and are confident that it has potential for great success. You can publish your work yourself without having to wait for another publisher's green light.

The Disadvantages of Self-Publishing

While the advantages of self-publishing are countless, there are many notable disadvantages that you must be aware of before venturing into the publishing world.

Title availability will be much smaller

Large publishing companies have pre-established relationships with distributors and stores. It is not difficult for a large publishing company to get, for instance, Barnes & Noble to carry one of its titles. As a self-publisher, you most likely do not have any pre-established relationships with distributors, bookstores, etc. You must start from scratch and build these relationships on your own. It will be more difficult and take more time for your book to become as widely available as it would with a large, pre-established publishing company.

Start-up costs

Because you are a new author releasing a new book from your new business, you must incur *all* of the start-up costs. You must put everything into place—paying for all new business licensing fees, hiring editors, paying for a cover design, paying for printing, securing storage areas for your books, purchasing an accounting program, purchasing a computer to run your accounting program, paying to take a class to learn how to use your computer and your accounting program—the list goes on. You must secure start-up capital that will allow you to create a solid, high quality, stable business. There will be many bumps in the road as you learn the publishing process. You do not want to have to stop production of your book because you ran out of funds and couldn't pay your graphic designer for your cover art.

Production and labor

You will have to manage each step of the production process of your book. No one will do it for you. As with a large publishing company, you will not be able to turn in a manuscript and weeks or months later, poof! It's a book. Every step of the way will require your hard work, blood, sweat and tears.

Relationships, relationships, relationships

You are new to the publishing and literary industry. Most likely, you don't know many people who are in the industry. You must do the research and relationship building from the ground, up. You do not have a list of trusted colleagues and patrons that you can draw upon at a moment's notice like large publishers. You can't call on a buyer at Borders and ask her if she would like to buy your latest book based on the successes of your previous published works. You must build relationships, earn trust and weed out the good from the bad based on your own experiences.

Being Business Minded

You've reviewed the advantages and disadvantages of self-publishing. You've weighed the pros and the cons. You've decided to self-publish! Great choice.

Now you must prepare yourself and get into the proper mindset for starting and running a successful business. You first must decide what your goals are. Do you want to sell your book and only your book? Do you want to start out with one book, then publish several more of your own? Do you want to eventually publish other authors?

Knowing your goals

Decide what your passions are. Create a mission statement for yourself that describes exactly what you hope to achieve. As you delve into publishing and field all of the curves and bumps in the road, your mission may become clouded, and you may forget that your ultimate goal and passion was, for instance, to publish a series of books detailing each specific variety of coffee bean. In the midst of the process of starting your coffee-bean publishing company, you find that space travel is becoming an increasingly popular subject and you consider capitalizing on the trends by writing and publishing a book on space travel. While variety is the spice of life, and learning new things is always good, you begin to lose sight of your original goal and don't understand why you can't get a good grasp on all of your subjects and your market.

Know your goals and your passions. Refer to your mission statement many times during the self-publishing process to remind you how and why you got here in the first place. Be careful not to get sidetracked by other endeavors that may seem promising but aren't linked to your areas of expertise and passion.

Preparing for success

Now that you have decided to move full steam ahead as a self-publisher, you must go into all of your ventures as if you are already a best-selling author. Readers are like bees and dogs; they can smell fear. If you go into the publishing business hesitant or scared, it will become apparent through the work that you produce and through your attitude and dealings with other associates and businesses in the publishing industry.

Part of success is also knowing when you need help. You can't be afraid to solicit help from qualified individuals. If you know nothing about accounting, you will need to hire someone who does. If you don't know the first thing about typesetting, you will have to hire an experienced typesetter that will turn the interior design of your book into a work of art. Don't be afraid to use some of your hard-earned money to pay your qualified staff. It is implausible to think that you will be able to do everything yourself. Don't be afraid to invest in others to improve upon your product.

Remaining stress free

Or, at least remain as stress free as you possibly can. With success almost always comes extremely hard work, dedication and stress. Starting a new business venture will be frightening, but you must not let your fear and stress get the best of you. That's why you have done your research and hired qualified staff; to take some of the stress off of yourself.

2

You've Got to Get Some Dough

I had just come home from serving seven years in federal prison. I didn't have a dime to my name, nor did I have anyone who wanted to give me money to pursue my dream.

Yeah, cash rules everything around us. Bottom line is this: you've got to get some money to make your dream into a reality. No one is going to help you. You have to help yourself. The first thing you have to realize is how do I get some money? Let me repeat that. How do I get some M-O-N-E-Y?

I wrote a letter to my friends, and family.

Then I waited. I waited for what seemed like forever.

By the next week, the money came in for my dream. I was on my way.

To My Dearest Friend(s):

If you have received this letter it is because I need your help. I am trying to raise the much-needed $2880 for the publishing of my first Novel. I am asking for donations for this project. The novel is finished, complete, finally done and sitting on my living room table in an envelope addressed to the printer. The only thing missing is the check to go into it. As my friend, you know that this Novel is my dream come true. It is my belief that this novel will bless others and warn them of the awful dangers of the drug game, in addition to reminding us of the power of God. He is a restorer and all of you (my friends) have watched God take me from embarrassment and separation, to RESTORATION. Please find it in your heart to help me by donating $100 to my cause. I will, of course, accept any amount, but I am requesting $100 from each of my friends to reach my eventual goal of $2880.
Please send a check made payable to BOOKMASTERS and mail to the below address.

I believe that I will receive the needed funding for this book. I thank you for all of your support, prayers, comments and encouragement. Soon, I will introduce the world to "Let That Be The Reason."

Sincerely,

Vickie M. Stringer
614-258-8611

Bookmasters
422 S. 18th Street
Columbus, Ohio 43205

Example of letter asking for financial assistane

Getting Start-up Capital

In order to start any business, self-publishing or other, you will need funding. You'll need a computer to type your manuscript.

You'll need paper and ink to print your manuscript. You'll need notebooks and pens to jot down your ideas for your self-publishing company. You had to buy this book to help you to start your self-publishing company, or you'll need to pay overdue fees to your library for keeping the book for so long. All of these things have something in common: they cost money. And this is just the very tip of the iceberg.

To run a successful publishing company, as you'll read in the following chapters, you will need to pay fees to obtain the necessary licensing to start your company; you'll utilize resources such as editors, typesetters and graphic artists; you'll have to pay to have your book printed; you'll need an accounting program to track your accounts payable and receivable; you'll need funds to fall back on when your distributors avoid payment; you will need to publicize and advertise. But right now, you need money just to *start.*

If you've kept true to the old adage "a penny saved is a penny earned," you may have a sizable chunk of savings that you can use for your start-up capital. Or, if you were the recipient of a large inheritance or you've recently won the lottery, you are well on your way.

However, if you're anything like the rest of us, you'll need assistance. There are countless ways to raise money to start your small publishing company, most commonly through a bank loan, grant, partnership or insurance policies.

Loans

If you are looking to get a loan to help fund the start your small publishing company, there are several different options available:

- Small Business Administration loans—Many who decide to start a small business of their own seek a loan through the Small Business Administration. For more information on how to receive funding through your local Small Business Administration, visit www.sba.gov.
- Bank loans—The traditional way to receive loans is through a bank. Unfortunately, many banks do not view small publishing companies as good candidates for loans. It is often easier to be approved for a home improvement loan or a vacation loan than it is to get a loan to start a small business, especially in self-publishing. Banks have seen many small businesses fail, and are reluctant to provide funding for a venture that they view to be risky. On the bright side, though, the more assets you have, the easier it will be to get a loan from a bank. Own a house? You may be able to use the equity from your home or take out a second mortgage to gain start-up capital for your small publishing company. Have any savings? Instead of spending your entire savings on starting your publishing company, use your savings to get a loan. Banks are more likely to lend to loan candidates who have a history of responsible spending and saving, i.e. your savings.

Grants

There are several grants available for funding small businesses and for artistic endeavors, such as from the National Endowment for the Arts. A simple search on Google.com will reveal many potential sources for available grant money to finance your small publishing company or to provide start-up capital.

Partnerships

Taking a partner in your business venture is another possible source for start-up capital and funding your publishing company. With a partner, you are no longer alone; you have someone else to share in the costs and responsibilities. A partner will also share in your successes, and could be an easy solution to your initial financial woes.

At the same time, sharing your business ventures with a partner is not hassle free. Not only do partners share in the finances and successes of your company, partners also share in the downfalls and failures of a company. Moreover, you and your partner are not exclusive. The decisions made by one partner affect the entire company. As quickly as a partner can provide you with funds, a partner can help you to lose your funds.

Insurance policies

If you possess whole life or annuity insurance, you may be able to borrow funds against your policy. With while life or annuity insurance, in addition to the insurance coverage, a cash value accumulates through your insurance company's investment in higher yielding mutual funds, stocks or bonds. For instance, if your policy is worth $10,000 with a $1,000 cash value, you can borrow up to $1,000 in cash. This amount is deducted from the value of your policy, so you are not necessarily required to repay the borrowed amount. Contact your insurance provider for more information about borrowing cash against your policy.

Getting Creative

If the conventional ways of raising start-up capital don't pan out, you must get creative. Many business owners have financed their business through unconventional means. If you have the motivation, drive and desire to succeed, you must come up with new ways to get money.

Networking

Networking is an essential concept throughout the entire self-publishing experience. In later chapters, you will learn how networking is essential in the production, sales, publicity and marketing arenas of self-publishing. Networking is equally, if not more, important in the beginning stages of funding your publishing company.

Networking – the process of meeting and communicating with others in your same area of interest for the purpose of mutual advancement – can be a lucrative avenue for financing. Getting to know others in the publishing industry can help you to learn who has money, who needs money, how money is earned and how it is spent.

Learn from those who were in your same position. Talk to successful self-publishers about how they financed their beginning stages and maintained their capital throughout their growth. Talk to and learn from less successful self-publishers about how they financed their beginning stages, how they attempted to maintain their capital and where they went wrong. Each self-publisher will have his or her own success and failure stories, and the more you ask, the more you will be able to learn from wise decisions or grave mistakes.

Learn from others' mistakes. It will be a lot cheaper than learning these lessons on your own.

In-kind services

In-kind services are the exchange of one service for another service, whether it be services in exchange for money, or the financial equivalent.

Through networking, you may be lucky enough to come across someone who is willing to provide you with services in exchange for discounted rates or another service. For instance, you may find a highly qualified editor who is willing to discount his or her rates in exchange for your referral to another client. Never underestimate the power and potential of in-kind services. If you can't compensate someone in the total monetary value, what can you provide? References, name credits, future opportunities with your company when it grows, credits on your Web site, the possibilities are endless.

Friends and Family

When all else fails—and it might—gaining your start-up capital through the kindness and generosity of your friends and family is another promising means of financing. Maybe you were blessed with an extremely large family or a wide circle of friends. Maybe you have a rich great-aunt. Hopefully, you didn't burn any important bridges before you decided to self-publish. If any of the above apply to you, you could be well on your way to obtaining your necessary start-up capital.

Don't be afraid to ask. You can't get what you don't ask for. Write your friends a letter. Call your closest family members on the phone, or better—pay them a visit. You may be surprised with the positive response and support that you receive.

Image

Before applying any of your get-money tactics, you must first have a product or at least a solid, firm idea for your product or a business plan. No one has ever approached a bank with nothing as far as preparation in hand and gotten a business loan. Networking with other publishers won't get you very far if you don't do your research and know the inner-workings of the business and its important players, and how you plan to make your mark in the publishing world. Family or friends will not likely help you to finance your business if you do not have any ideas or products to present to them.

Do your research. From the very beginning stages you are creating an image. Your book, your self, your business is a brand; an image. When selling any product, you must project an image of success, even if you haven't gotten so much as a manuscript. If you have an idea, and you want to sell your idea, you must project a positive image.

Do your research

The quest for financing is like a constant interview. If you are unprepared, your interviewers will sense it. No one wants to invest time or money into a venture that is not well thought out, well-planned and well-researched. When approaching a person or institution for funding, you must appear knowledgeable, confident and emitting an air of success, even if you haven't started anything yet. You must convince others that their time and money will be well spent and will be a worthwhile investment.

- ❖ Knowing the industry—Know the industry, its important players and the history. The more you know about self-publishing, the more your concept will be respected, not to mention that it will help in the development and publishing of your book. Invest in a subscription to *Publishers Weekly* magazine.
- ❖ Knowing your work – Know your own work. If you're publishing a children's book, be very familiar with the other books and authors in the children's literature arena.

Know how your work compares with others'. Is your idea similar to someone else's? Do you have an innovative idea that will create a new niche in children's literature? The more you know about your genre and the other related books, authors and publishers, the more you will subsequently know about your own work, and how you will choose to compare to the others.

- Knowing business – Research distributors, wholesalers, libraries, supermarkets, specialty stores, bookstores. Know the practices and policies of every place where you hope to sell your book. If you are publishing a book about football, you will want your book to appear on the shelves at a bookstore, but also at a specialty store, such as a sporting goods store. The practices of getting your book into a traditional bookstore as opposed to a sporting goods store are vastly different. The more you know about practices and policies, the faster and more efficient you will be able to break into that market.

Your research and learning will probably never end, but once you are sufficiently knowledgeable of the angles of the publishing industry, you must create a business plan. Whether it is an elaborate multi-paged plan that is larger than your book itself, or a short summary of your goals, you must have a clear and concise idea of how you will operate and run your self-publishing company.

Creating a detailed and well thought-out business plan will not only help you to determine budgeting, expenses and organize your schedule of events, it is a great way to show potential funders that you are serious about your company and are prepared and informed of the necessary steps to make your company a success.

Presentation

Presentation is everything, especially in the publishing industry. Your product is essentially nothing but presentation.

Even if you have the most elaborate, detailed, fool-proof business plan, if it is presented poorly, none of the content will matter. Imagine that someone has asked you to fund his or her project or business. What would you need that person do for you in order for you to be convinced?

Always emit confidence. You must appear to already be a success, even if you have yet to sell one book. Professionalism, confidence and knowledge are power, and very reassuring traits to a person or institution that is considering providing funding.

When you have high-quality presentation and a solid image and brand no one will be able to tell if you are working out of a corner office with a view or from your kitchen table.

3

How to Set Up Your Company

I had read several books on how to start a company. Unfortunately, none of the books fit my personal situation. So, I personalized everything pertaining to what would work best for me. I learned the hard way that I couldn't work with friends and family—I'm sorry. It is one thing to have friends and family in your corner to support you, but business, family and friends should never mix, if possible.

Set your company up and build it strong, because the foundation you lay today will be the successful business that stands on it tomorrow.

Ask yourself this question. If I were to become a success, what would the foundation need to be like? No matter how silly you think you will look, organize your company for success. For instance, I had a warehouse with one title. Today, I've outgrown that warehouse by six times.

Business Structure

As a self-publisher, you are creating your own company and your own business. Now that you have your start-up capital, you need to determine what kind of company you want to start. Choosing the proper type of business structure is dependent on your current and future goals.

It is also recommended that you consult a business attorney when choosing your business structure.

Sole Proprietorship

If you choose no other business structure, your business is, by default, a sole proprietorship. This business structure is often the simplest type of structure to set up and to operate for a self-publisher. By definition, in a sole proprietorship, you and your business are one. There is no separation between the individual and the business. *You* are the business and the business is *you.*

Partnership

When you decide to pair with one or more persons in starting your business, you form a partnership.

An advantage to a partnership is that you have another person/persons to share in the start-up costs, responsibility and successes. However, a partnership can become tricky as each partner is responsible for the finances of the entire partnership. For instance, if your partner is in charge of advertising, and goes into deep debt over advertising costs, you are also responsible for this debt even though you feel you had nothing to do with this aspect of the business.

Corporation

If you set up a corporation, you become an employee of that corporation. You are not one with the corporation, as you would be in a sole proprietorship.

This type of structure can become costly, as more in-depth accounting, higher taxes, paperwork, etc. can be involved. However, if for some reason your corporation becomes involved in a legal suit, employees are likely not liable. Consequently, the corporation can be sued, but most often employees' personal assets are not involved.

Limited Liability Company

Limited liability is becoming an increasingly popular business structure. A limited liability company can be less costly and less complicated than a corporation but with many of the same benefits. Like a corporation, you may not be personally liabilities incurred by other people associated with your company.

Taxes

Not only will you have to pay taxes on the income that you earn, you will have to deal with sales tax as well. Consult a professional tax adviser or attorney regarding both income taxes and sales taxes. The last thing that you want is for Uncle Sam to come after you for improperly filing income or sales taxes.

For details on how to file your taxes in each of these business structures, visit the IRS Web site at www.irs.gov or consult a tax attorney.

Income taxes

Your calculation, payments and filing times will be dependent upon the business structure that you choose for your self-publishing company. You may only have to file taxes yearly, with your personal income tax return, or you may be required to file quarterly. Keep these points in mind when choosing a business structure.

Accurate accounting records are essential to ensure the proper filing of your income taxes. Secure an accurate and reliable accounting system after choosing your business structure. Whether you are hiring a professional accountant or utilizing a program such as Quicken, QuickBooks or Peachtree Accounting, you must have a thorough understanding of the system in order to keep the organized and precise financial records that are vital to filing income taxes.

Deductions

On the bright side, depending on the business structure you choose, many of the costs of publishing are tax-deductible, such as marketing costs, printing costs and costs directly related to your book's production including writing, editing and typesetting.

If you use a portion of your house or apartment as your office, you may also be eligible to deduct a portion of your rent, utilities, furniture, office supplies and equipment used exclusively for business purposes.

Discuss tax deductions with your financial adviser or attorney. You may be surprised to learn the many ways that you can deduct your expenses!

Sales tax

Sales taxes, unlike income taxes, are not taxes that you must file at a certain point in time each year. Sales tax laws differ from state to state. Visit www.irs.gov or your state government's own Web site for more information.

In many states, if you make a retail sale to an individual in your own state, you will have to collect a sales tax which you will later have to repay to your state.

However, for the most part, if your sales are mostly to distributors, wholesalers or bookstores, you will not have to worry about implementing sales tax on your own. Sales tax is often charged to the end user, meaning that in most cases, the reader who purchases your book from a bookstore will pay the sales tax. The bookstore will be responsible for charging the sales tax.

You will be responsible for paying sales tax to your state, so make it a priority to become familiar with your state's sales tax policies.

Licensing

The necessary licensing will also be dependent on the business structure that you choose for your company. Check with your local chamber of commerce to find out what licenses are required for your company. Through networking, learn from someone in your community who has already gone through the process of starting and licensing a small business.

Sales tax license

Depending on your state's requirements, you may need to apply for a sales tax license, resale permit or state tax ID number. Visit your state government's Web site or sales tax office for more information on licensing requirements specific to your state.

Knowing the Law

In order to operate within any industry, you must first be aware and well-versed in the laws and regulations of the industry.

The First Amendment of the U.S. Constitution states:

> *Congress shall make no law respecting an establishment of religion, or prohibiting the free exercise thereof; or abridging the freedom of speech, or of the press; or the right of the people peaceably to assemble, and to petition the Government for a redress of grievances.*

However, the First Amendment is not without its rules and regulations. A few of the most important laws regarding publishing are copyright and libel laws.

Copyright laws

The copyright laws protect your work from being duplicated by others, and protect others' work from being duplicated by you. See Chapter 4 for more information on how to secure copyrights for your work.

Libel

In Webster's dictionary, libel is defined as "a written or oral defamatory statement or representation that conveys an unjustly unfavorable impression; a statement or representation published without just cause and tending to expose another to public contempt."

Libel laws state that it is illegal to publish an untrue and defamatory statement about an individual that causes harm to the individual's reputation.

In other words, if you were to publish a statement about a specific person that is blatantly false and causes measurable damage to that person's reputation, this could constitute as libel and you could possibly be sued.

To learn more about libel laws in the United States, visit http://usinfo.state.gov.

Plagiarism

In Webster's dictionary, plagiarism is defined as "to steal and pass off the ideas or words of another as one's own; use another's production without crediting the source."

You may not copy any portion of another's work without the proper crediting and documentation.

Naming your Company

Another very important process in your company's development is choosing a name for your company. It is common for self-publishers to use their own names to title their companies, but you may decide to choose a more creative title for your company that conveys a larger, more powerful image. Whatever you choose to name your company, research to be sure that no other publishing or similar company is already using the name. Choose a name that is easy to spell, and keep in mind that you will be using that name for your Web address as well. Long, difficult-to-spell names often prove difficult to locate on the Internet through search engines. Names that are difficult to pronounce will be hard to remember and may be difficult to promote. Choose a name with which you can identify, and a name in which you can take pride. The name will represent your company for its entire history. Choose something unique, simple and unforgettable.

Your company logo

Your company's logo is equally as important as your company's name. Your logo represents your company and you. An effective logo will be recognized by the consumer even in your company name's absence. Just like your company name, your logo should be unique, simple and unforgettable. You will have to reproduce your logo many times, on your Web site, on your books' covers, on your company letterhead, etc. Refer to *The 22 Immutable Laws of Branding* by Al Ries and Laura Ries for more history and useful strategy in branding your company through the use of a logo.

Your place of business

Securing your place of business and contact information is another crucial step in developing your company. In order to create your business structure, obtain necessary licensing and perform virtually every other aspect of business, you must secure the necessary contact information and means of communication.

- Utilizing a P.O. Box—If you are not utilizing a separate office space to start your company, you will want to consider applying for a post office box as a means of receiving your mail. If you are working out of your home, a P.O. Box will allow you to keep your personal home address from becoming public knowledge.
- Fax, phone, e-mail, Internet—Having a fax line, a phone line and an e-mail address is crucial to communication in all aspects of your business. Distributors may want to fax in their orders. You will certainly need a phone line that can make both local and long distance calls, for promotional, sales and all other business purposes. Customers and fans may choose to reach you through e-mail. E-mail is much faster than regular USPS mail, and much cheaper than a long-distance phone call. Internet access is fun-

damental in applying for necessary licenses, ISBNs, bar codes, researching distributors and wholesalers, finding book reviewers and receiving online orders through your company Web site.

4

Production/ Getting Listed

Finally, I had obtained all the cash I needed, and now, it was time to produce my book. As most self-publishers can testify, it was a large undertaking to publish my first book. Not only was I nervous about bringing out a book, I knew that I wanted everything to turn out perfectly. As to be expected, everything didn't go right, but, as a result, I learned to become flexible.

Oh, where do I begin? How do you find that team who gives your book that look, that finish and that packaging? How do you bring together the team who makes it

all happen? Editing, typesetting, cover design, contacts, the list goes on.

So how do you find qualified people for production of your book? Yeah, the production. It's like preparing for a performance—gather your cast and select them carefully. Trial and error is a good thing. Learn to laugh at yourself and never give up.

Remember, it's your time to shine. Introduce your book to the world. What you see is what you get!

What Does the Production Process Entail?

The production process includes all of the steps that you must take in order to turn your work from a manuscript into a book. It includes editing, typesetting, cover design, the copyrighting process, applying for an ISBN, bar code, LCCN, printing and everything in between.

The success and image of your book depends on the success of the production process. It is important to remember not to rush any aspect of production. Although it may be tempting to rush one step or another in order to get your book printed faster and out on the market quicker, your success will only be as good as your product.

Writing, Rewriting, Revising

You will likely make several changes to your manuscript throughout each step of the production process. Many new authors believe that once they have finished writing their manuscript, they will not have to make any more changes to it. After all, it only seems logical that after spending months and years completing your manuscript, you probably don't want to spend much more time writing and rewriting the content. However, you must be willing to change and improve your product at all times and during all stages of production. It is important to remember that you must always be willing to write, rewrite and revise.

Editing

After you have written your manuscript, the next step in production is editing. Almost every manuscript, whether it is fiction or non-fiction, children's book or cookbook, needs to be edited for content and grammar.

There are three different types of editing in the book industry: copy editing, content editing and book-doctoring. When hiring editors, it is crucial that you obtain credentials and samples of work that they have done in the past. Many people underestimate the difficulty of editing, and someone who has not had the proper training or qualifications may feel that he or she can edit your book anyway. Be wary of any editor who can not produce credentials, references and samples, especially if you do not have an extensive background yourself on the latest grammar, literary style guides and industry standards. When interviewing editors, it is often beneficial to ask candidates to edit a writing sample of your choice to check for thoroughness and understanding of your tone.

It is also beneficial to choose an editor/editors who are experienced in your subject of work. If you are writing a children's book, it will be very difficult for an editor to improve on the story's content if he or she has little to no prior experience with what makes a successful or unsuccessful children's book.

Get to know the other books in your related field. Thoroughly read and review them to decide what you like and dislike about each one. Use these as samples to give your editors direction and to create a solid idea in your own mind of how you want your book to look and read.

The copy editor

A copy editor looks for grammatical errors in your manuscript. A copy editor will ensure correct subject/verb agreement and consistent tense usage. He or she will correct improper use of apostrophes and commas and make certain that all proper nouns are capitalized. A copy editor should be familiar with the different styles of writing and editing. A good copy editor and also a thorough author should always have the latest edition of the MLA Handbook, AP Style Guide, Chicago Manual of Style or other writing or editing guide on his or her desk at all times. Be sure that your copy editor is familiar with these specific handbooks, as they are standard in the industry. When the typesetting of your book is completed, it will also be necessary for a copy editor to review the book one final time before going to print, to guarantee the text is as error-free as possible.

To illustrate the function of a copy editor, take this un-edited sentence:

See spot run

A copy editor will make sure that the proper punctuation appears at the end of the sentence (a period). A copy editor would also capitalize the 's' in "spot", as it is a proper noun. After the copy editor is finished with this sentence, it should read:

See Spot run.

The content editor

Unlike the copy editor, the content editor is not as concerned with grammar as he or she is with the content of your work. A content editor ensures that your story line remains consistent, you have strong character development, there are no holes in your plot line, the setting of the story is concrete and the chapter breakdown flows properly. A content editor will work closely with the author and may review the manuscript several times to guarantee consistency and quality.

Again, take the sentence:

> See Spot run.

To improve upon this sentence, the content editor would tell you, the author, to define the details and bring out the imagery in the sentence to create a more vivid picture in your readers' imaginations. A content editor might ask: what color are Spot's spots? Where is Spot running? Is Spot a he or a she? After the content editor is finished with this sentence, it might read:

> See Spot, the pure-bred champion Dalmatian male, with his stunning black spots perfectly off-set by his brilliantly white coat, sprinting down the avenue after the dazzlingly red fire truck.

The book doctor

The role of the book doctor differs from the copy editor and the content editor, as the book doctor's primary concern is the manuscript's "big picture". A book doctor's role is to evaluate the manuscript in its entirety and suggest how it can be improved as a whole. A book doctor will tell you if he or she hates the ending of your book and will tell you how to make it better. A book doctor will tell you if your main character will be unappealing to readers, and will tell you how you can make your main character more likeable and relatable to your audience. A book doctor's purpose is to be brutally honest about the strengths and flaws in your book and at the same time will tell you how you can use these strengths and flaws to make your book truly fantastic. A book doctor is like a best friend who will tell you if the outfit you are wearing makes you look fat, old and unappealing, but also gives you solid, concrete options on what to change and what to wear that will look most flattering and make you irresistible to your audience.

Once again, let's take a look at the sentence:

> See Spot run.

A book doctor will ask: Does this sentence work here? Is this the best way to develop the story? When a book doctor is done with this sentence, he or she may say:

> Having Spot run here does not make sense. Instead of running, Spot should be having an affair with the neighbor dog who already has illegitimate puppies with Spot's dying half-brother.

Time and cost

You may be able to find one editor who can serve all three purposes—copy editor, content editor and book doctor. Nevertheless, this is often not the case. You must allow enough time and funds to complete the editing process. Editing costs vary greatly, as they are dependent on the amount of work that needs to be put into your manuscript, the number of pages of your manuscript and the number of changes that the editor makes. Generally, editors can charge from $200 to $2,000, also dependent on the editor's level of experience and expertise, and may charge on a per-project or per-page basis.

The time it takes to edit a manuscript also is dependent on the length and changes that must be made to the manuscript. Generally, each editor may take anywhere from one week to one month to edit a manuscript.

Inquire about your editor's procedures. Does the editor want a hard copy of the manuscript to read and edit, or does he or she edit from an electronic copy saved on a disk? Will the editor input the changes, or will you be responsible for inputting your own edits? Be sure you are clear on the editor's methods and processes so that you may allow the correct amount of time to complete the procedure before moving on to the next step in production.

Typesetting

After your manuscript has been edited, and all of your changes have been made and saved to an electronic file, you can begin the typesetting process. Typesetting is the art of designing a book's interior. It encompasses the page layout, font, spacing, headers, footers, page numbers, chapter headings, etc.

It is possible to perform your own typesetting with the use of a computer program such as QuarkXPress or Pagemaker. If you are familiar with these programs, you may be able to save the time and money that it will take to find a qualified professional typesetter. However, if you do not have previous experience with the use of these programs, it will be beneficial to you to hire a professional typesetter.

As with finding an editor, it is essential that you review the credentials and work samples of your prospective typesetters. An experienced, professional typesetter will have completed many projects before yours, and will be able to provide you with samples of other books that he or she has typeset.

Also as with editing, it will benefit you to research the interior design of other books that you have read. Take note of the aspects of the design in other books that you like and those that you dislike. Be sure to make your preferences clear to your typesetter, and be sure that you are satisfied with the look of the final product.

Time and cost

Dependent on the experience and expertise of the typesetter and the length of your manuscript, typesetting services can range from $200 - $1,000 and will take anywhere from 1 day to 2 weeks to complete. Your typesetter may charge on a per-project or hourly basis.

If any changes need to be made to your manuscript after the typesetter has completed the layout, additional charges may apply.

Cover Design

Your book's cover design is perhaps the most important aspect of marketing your book. Buyers and readers base their first impressions on the cover of your book. It is best to hire a professional graphic designer to create your book cover. This process can be done during the time that the editing and typesetting process is taking place.

Your graphic designer will create both the front and back covers of your book, and will lay the text for your title and byline on the front cover, and your synopsis, blurbs and any other information that you want to include on the back cover.

As always, be sure that your graphic designer is experienced and has solid credentials and work samples to present to you. Present specific ideas of what you want your cover design to look like, and gauge the designer's willingness to work with you to improve on your ideas and create several different samples from which you can choose.

Be sure you are aware of the graphic designer's policies. If you are dissatisfied with the cover, will the designer be willing to make changes to his or her finished product? If you want to change the text that has already been laid on the cover, will your designer be cooperative? Will there be fees involved for making changes?

Time and cost

Depending on the complexity of the cover design and the experience, time and efforts used by the designer, your cover can range from $300 to $3,000 and may take anywhere between a few days to a month to be completed.

Contracts

It is common to sign a contract with any freelance employee that you hire to assist you in the production process. Thoroughly review all contracts before signing and keep a copy for your own records. It is advisable to review any contracts with your lawyer, and even to ask your lawyer to help you draft a contract or confidentiality agreement that your freelance employees will sign for you.

How to Find Qualified People

Word-of-mouth

Do you know someone who knows someone? Check all credentials before entrusting a portion of the outcome of your book to someone. Even if your best friend swears by a certain editor, you must check credentials and be confident in the abilities of your employees. What may have worked for someone else may not be the same thing that will work for you.

Advertisements

Another way to locate qualified and cost-efficient personnel is through newspaper advertisements or placing a job listing with your local college or university's newspaper or Web site. Contact a trusted institution's career services office to place a job listing in a campus newspaper or Web site. These listings are often free, and many times you can create more than one listing. Guidance counselors may be able to assist you in finding individuals in your target area of need. The goal of colleges and universities is to gainfully employ as many of their students as possible. Guidance counselors are often very cooperative in pairing students with job opportunities, creating win – win situations for all parties involved.

Getting Listed

The next step in the production process getting your book listed. There are various numbers and lists that you must obtain for your book so that it is easily accessible by readers, easy to purchase and easy to locate on different literary databases.

Pricing your Book

There are many factors that you must consider when pricing your book. You must be profitable and make enough money with your book sales in order to cover all of the costs of production, plus more. However, you don't want to price your book too high, turning your potential readers off and driving them toward a less expensive book.

The first step in pricing your book is to know your market and to be familiar with how a similar book in your market is priced. Other factors that must be considered when pricing your book are whether your book is a hard cover or paperback, if you intend to include photographs or illustrations in your book, if these photos and illustrations are in color, if you are going to use high gloss paper, etc.

Factoring in all costs including cost of production, book quality, size and content, each book should be priced at a minimum of 8 times the cost that it takes to produce your book. For example, after you have evaluated all costs and you come to the conclusion that each book will cost you approximately $2.50 to produce, you should price your book at $20.00, minimum.

Once you have decided on a price that you are comfortable with, be sure to include the price on every ISBN, Bar code or any other application that asks for pricing. Also, *remember to display the price on the book.* This seems simple, but is a mistake that has been made many times by many authors. If you don't display the price on the book, readers will not know how much it will cost. Your book will appear unprofessional and will not be taken seriously.

The ISBN

An ISBN, or International Standard Book Number, is your book's ID number. The ISBN should be printed both on the copyright page of your book and on the book's back cover above the bar code.

An ISBN currently contains 10 digits broken into four parts. The first series of numbers identifies your book by geographic location, the second is a unique number assigned to each publisher, the third denotes a specific title or edition and the fourth is a check digit that validates the ISBN.

However, in 2007, ISBNs will change into 13 digit numbers to include the EAN/Bar code prefix 978. Books printed before 2007 will not require new ISBNs, just the inclusion of the EAN prefix.

For more information on the 13 digit conversion, visit www.isbn.org.

How to obtain an ISBN

You can obtain an ISBN from the R.R. Bowker company by visiting www.isbn.org and filling out an online application (*please see following page for sample of application*). ISBNs come in blocks of 10, 100, 1,000 and 10,000. If you buy ISBNs in a block of 10, this means that you have enough ISBNs for 10 titles or editions. These can be saved for other books that you wish to publish in the future.

The cost of obtaining ISBNs varies, and is dependent on processing fees, number of ISBNs you purchase and the promptness in which you wish to receive them. For a price listing, visit www.isbn.org.

Upon ordering ISBNs, you will receive your block of numbers along with an electronic ISBN log sheet. The electronic log sheet is provided for the benefit of keeping track of which ISBN of the block corresponds with which title or edition, and can be e-mailed or couriered to you usually within 24 hours to 10 business days.

If you decide to produce different versions or editions of your book, you will need to assign a separate ISBN for each version. For instance, if you are publishing a hard cover and a paperback version of your book, you will need to assign each a different ISBN. The same is true if you decide to create an audio book, or if you print a revised version of that contains significant changes.

The Bar Code

Bar codes are important for the sale of your book. Just like a UPC

APPLICATION FOR AN ISBN PUBLISHER PREFIX

INTERNATIONAL STANDARD BOOK NUMBER--UNITED STATES AGENCY
International Standard Numbering System for the Information Industry
630 Central Avenue, New Providence, New Jersey 07974
Email: isbn-san@bowker.com FAX: 908-219-0188
R.R. Bowker LLC, a Cambridge Information Group company

International Standard ISO 2108

APPLICATION FOR AN ISBN PUBLISHER PREFIX

FOR AGENCY USE ONLY

SYMBOL: ____________________

PREFIX: ____________________

PLEASE PRINT OR TYPE:

Company/Publisher Name: ____________________

Address: ____________________

City: ____________ State: ____________ Zip ____________

Phone Number: ____________________ Do Not Publish: ___

Fax Number: ____________________ Do Not Publish: ___

Toll Free Number: ____________________

E-MAIL: ____________________ Do Not Publish: ___

Web Site: ____________________

Fax-on-Demand: ____________ Toll Free Fax: ____________

If P.O. Box Indicated, Local Street Address is Required:

Name of Rights & and Permissions Contact: ____________________

Title: ____________ Phone Number: ____________

Name of ISBN Coordinator/Contact: ____________________

Title: ____________ Phone Number: ____________

Division/Subsidiary of: ____________________

APPLICATION FOR AN ISBN PUBLISHER PREFIX

(circle which one and provide company name)

Imprints: ____________________

PUBLISHING INFORMATION:

1. Indicate year you started publishing: ____________________

2. Indicate what type of products you produce (circle):

   o Books   o Videos   o Spoken Words on Cassette/CD
   o Software   o E-books

   Other - Please specify: ____________________

3. Book Subject Area (circle):

   o Children's
   o Law
   o Medical
   o Religious
   o Sci-Tech
   o Other - Please specify: ____________________

DISTRIBUTION INFORMATION:

1. Do you distribute for, or are you distributed by, any other company?
   Yes: ________ No: ________. If yes, please provide full company name, address and ISBN Publisher Prefix (if any):

   ____
   ____
   ____

PAYMENT: A NON-REFUNDABLE PROCESSING SERVICE CHARGE
(Service charge fees are subject to change)
EXPRESS PROCESSING SURCHARGE $125
PRIORITY PROCESSING SURCHARGE $75

Please note: There is a Publisher Registration Fee. The fee will be charged to your **in addition to your selected processing fee,** and the total will be reflected on the The Publisher Registration Fee is as follows:
$24.95 10 ISBNs; $59.95 100 ISBNs; $174.95 1000 ISBNs; $399.95 10,00

For your convenience, an electronic copy of your ISBN log book will be stored on Bowker's BowkerLink website (a copy of your log book will also be e-mailed to you if requested). See attachment to application for further information.

ISBN PREFIX	EXPRESS PROCESSING FEE	PRIORITY PROCESSING FEE	REGULAR PROCESSING FEE
10 ISBNs	$350.00	$300.00	$225.00
100 ISBNs	$925.00	$875.00	$800.00
1,000 ISBNs	$1,325.00	$1,275.00	$1,200.00
10,000 ISBNs	-	-	$3,000.00

Annual Online Service Fee of $25: There is an annual fee for continuing access to yo However, your first year online log book service set up is **free**.

Reprinted with permission of R.R. Bowker LLC. Copyright 2005. All prices subject to change at any time.

symbol, a Bar code is used for the pricing of your book and for tracking the book's sales. It is located on the back cover of the book and displays the ISBN and the price.

How to obtain a Bar code

A Bar code can also be obtained from the R.R. Bowker company, or from many other companies such as Film Masters. To apply for a Bar code, you can simply visit the company's Web site, or you can even apply at the same time as you purchase your ISBN with an online application from www.isbn.org.

The cost of a Bar code also varies dependent on the number of Bar codes that you purchase and processing fees, but usually cost between $20 - $25 per Bar code.

A Bar code can be placed on the back cover of your book by your printer or your cover designer. You can have your Bar code sent to you electronically by your Bar code company, however it is suggested that you request the Bar code be sent directly to your printer, who will then open the file and place the Bar code on the back cover of your book digitally. By having your Bar code sent directly to the printer, you avoid the possibility of opening and corrupting the file. If you prefer to have your Bar code e-mailed or mailed to you, do not open the file. Instead, forward the file directly to your printer.

The LCCN

An LCCN, or Library of Congress Control Number, is another number that is assigned to your work. Unlike the ISBN, you need only one LCCN for every version of your work.

An LCCN guarantees that your book will be listed in the Library of Congress' database. This is especially important for sales to libraries, as many use the Library of Congress' database to order their books. The LCCN must also appear on the copyright page of your book, along with the ISBN.

To obtain an LCCN, you must first apply for a PCN—Preassigned Control Number. When the publishing process is complete, your PCN will become an LCCN. However, because your book has technically not yet been published at the time of application, the Library of Congress considers the number as pre-assigned. "Pre" meaning pre-publication.

You can apply for a PCN by visiting the Library of Congress' Web site at http://pcn.loc.gov/pcn. Upon approval of your PCN application, the Library of Congress will assign a PCN to your book. Applying for a PCN is free.

After completion of the application process, you will receive your PCN in an average of one to two weeks.

Printing

Now your production process is complete—you have had your manuscript edited, typeset and your cover design is complete. You have obtained all of the necessary numbers and information that needs to be displayed on your book. You have displayed the price of your book either on the back cover of your book (for paperbacks) or on the inside front cover of your book (for hard covers). You are ready to send your book to the printer.

Printing your book can take anywhere from 4 to 8 weeks, dependent on the type of book and the number of books that you wish to print. Be sure take this time into consideration when planning advertisements, listings and shipment of orders.

Choosing the right printer is crucial to the success and longevity of your book. While the popularity of self-publishing has increased tremendously over the past decade, more and more printers are popping up in order to meet the demand of the self-publishing authors. Many of these printers may not be capable of producing the quality of book that you desire.

As with your other laborers, it is common practice to research the credentials of your printer. Visit your printer's Web site and ask for samples of previously printed work. Peruse these samples for paper and ink quality, thickness of cover and sturdiness of the binding. Again, research other books in your field and choose a few to use as positive and negative samples of print quality. The quality of your printing will determine the level of professionalism in your work, can make or break a first impression and will determine how well and for how long you can keep several copies of your book in storage. If the cover's color quality is poor, it is possible that the colors will fade over time. If the binding is insufficient, your book may fall apart after minor wear and tear.

Request quotes and samples from your printer and compare the cost and quality (*please see the following pages for a sample quote request from www.Malloy.com*). With any printer, the more books you print, the lower the cost will be for each book. For instance, if you choose a print run of 500 paperback books, you may pay $2.50 per book, for a total of $1,250. However, if you choose a print run of 3,000 paperback books, you may pay $1.50 per book, for a total of $4,500.

I recommend Malloy Incorporated, a family-owned book printer based in Ann Arbor, Michigan. Malloy has been printing books

Quote Request

Consultative Estimating
You can request a quote by completing and submitting the form on this page. Our Pricing staff will review the specifications and provide an estimate, sometimes with a suggestion to consider other options based on their manufacturing expertise. Our goal is to return your quote within 24 hours to help make your print purchase decision just a little easier.

Contact Information

Name

Company

Address

City/State/ZIP

Email

Phone

Fax

Return quote via:

- (•) Email
- ( ) Fax
- ( ) Phone
- ( ) U.S. Mail

Background Information

How did you learn about our home page?

Has Malloy quoted for you in the past? ( ) Yes ( ) No

How many titles per year do you publish?

When do you need this quotation?

When will this job be sent to the printer?

What is your desired ship date?

Estimate Overview

Title

Quantities

Page Count

Trim Size

- (•) 5-1/2 x 8-1/2
- ( ) 6 x 9
- ( ) 7-3/8 x 9-1/4
- ( ) 8-1/2 x 11
- ( ) Other

(4-1/4 x 6 up to 10 x 12)

Electronic Quote Request

Text

Text Prep
- (•) PDF Files (preferred)
- ( ) Postscript Files
- ( ) Application Files
- ( ) CRC
- ( ) Other: ____

Text Proof
- (•) Yes
- ( ) No

Text Ink
- (•) 1/c
- ( ) 2/c

Text Stock
- **45#** ( ) White ( ) Offwhite ( ) Groundwood
- **50#** (•) White ( ) Offwhite ( ) Groundwood
- **60#** ( ) White ( ) Offwhite
- ( ) Other: ____

(See available stock)

Cover (for soft cover books)

Cover Prep
- ( ) Application Files (preferred)
- ( ) PDF File
- ( ) Color separated film
- ( ) Furnished cover (skip to binding section)

Cover Ink
- ( ) 1/c
- ( ) 2/c
- ( ) 3/c
- ( ) 4/c

Cover Coat
- ( ) Gloss U.V.
- ( ) Matte U.V.
- ( ) Gloss Film Lamination
- ( ) Matte Film Lamination
- ( ) Precision Spot Gloss

Cover Stock
- ( ) 10 pt. C1S
- ( ) 12 pt. C1S
- ( ) Other ____

(See available stock)

Case (for hard cover books)

Case Material ____

Endsheets
- ( ) Matching
- ( ) Printed

Boards
- ( ) 88 pt
- ( ) 98 pt

Stamping
- [ ] Spine

Electronic Quote Request (cont.)

- [ ] Cover 1
- [ ] Cover 4

If your adhesive case book will have a printed cover:

Case Ink	○ 1/c ○ 2/c ○ 3/c ○ 4/c
Case Coating	○ Gloss U.V. ○ Matte U.V. ○ Gloss Film Lamination ○ Matte Film Lamination ○ Precision Spot Gloss

Jacket (if applicable)

Jacket Stock	○ 80# C1S Enamel ○ Other [ ]
Jacket Ink	○ 1/c ○ 2/c ○ 3/c ○ 4/c
Jacket Coating	○ Gloss U.V. ○ Matte U.V. ○ Gloss Film Lamination ○ Matte Film Lamination ○ Precision Spot Gloss

Bind

Bind Style	◉ Perfect ○ Saddle stitch ○ RepKover(TM) - layflat paperback ○ Adhesive case ○ Other [ ]
Bind Options	☐ Perforate text ☐ Drill
Shrinkwrap	◉ None ○ In Singles ○ Conveniently

Other Information

Other [ ]

[Request Quote] [Reset Form]

Electronic Quote Request (cont.)

since 1960, and prints all of Triple Crown Publications' titles. Malloy is a one-stop printer, meaning it completes the entire printing process—from prepress to storage and fulfillment—on location. This is time and cost efficient, as many self-publishers find that much of the extra time, cost and headache when it comes to printing results from companies outsourcing various duties, and the inability to perform all tasks in-house.

Initial print run

It is easy to get caught in the trap of printing more books for less money. Evaluate your start-up capital, and project how many books you will be able to sell compared to how many books you will be able to store.

A good initial print run is 2,500 books. This will allow you enough books to sell without having to re-print right away. On the other hand, this will probably not be so many that you will be stuck with cases upon cases that you will have to store for an indefinite period of time.

Paper

You may have noticed that different books are comprised of several different types of paper. Some sheets are thicker than others, while some appear in different shades of white or gray. Printers carry a variety of different colors, thicknesses and types of paper, and samples can be provided for your review.

Paper is priced based upon its thickness. You can choose a cheaper type of paper such as newsprint, or opt for an expensive textured paper. The paper that you will choose will be dependent on the type of book that you are publishing. If you choose to publish a book of photography, you may want a thicker, gloss-coated book stock.

Again, research paper among other books that you know and like. Compare the paper with the samples provided by your printer, and choose based on cost and quality.

Binding

- Perfect binding – Perfect binding is the method in which Triple Crown Publications' books are bound. Perfect binding, as opposed to saddle stitch binding, consists of adhering pages with glue. The pages of your book's text are stacked and folded, creating a spine. The book's cover is then wrapped around the pages and glued onto the spine. Perfect binding is advantageous because it is cost efficient and also creates a squared spine on which text can be displayed. When a reader browses through a bookstore, the squared spine is what is often first seen. The square spine allows the title and author's name to be displayed, so when the books are stacked on the shelves of a store, your book's information is easily identifiable.
- Saddle stitch binding—Saddle stitch binding, unlike perfect binding, consists of securing pages with metal staples. Many brochures, catalogs and booklets are secured with saddle stitch binding. If your text is less than 100 pages, saddle stitch binding can be quick, easy and cost efficient. However, because of the metal staples, rust is common and discoloration of pages can occur.
- RepKover™ lay flat—Lay flat binding is what you might commonly see used in hard cover books with several pages, such as a dictionary; or very wide pages, such as in a children's picture book. In lay flat binding, pages are secured with glue, however the book's cover is not glued directly to the spine. You may have noticed in a dictionary or a children's book that there is a small gap between the

pages of text and the cover. This allows the book to "lay flat" on a table or other surface so that the pages will stay open without the reader holding them down.

Trim Sizes
Trim size refers to the measurements and dimensions of your book. Standard trim sizes include:

5½ x 8½
6 x 9
7 ⅜ x 9¼
8½ x 11

Fiction books and hard cover non-fiction books are commonly trimmed to 5 ½ x 8 ½ , while specialty books such as cookbooks, travel guides, books of photography or children's books are much larger. Conversely, romance novels and mass-market paperbacks can often have a smaller trim size. Research the trim sizes of other books in your genre and choose the size that you believe will best represent your book. Check with your printer to learn about the trim sizes that are offered.

Jackets
Hard cover books are often covered with jackets, also called dust jackets. These are used to protect your books' covers from damage, but are primarily utilized for the glossy, aesthetic value.

There are several different types of book jackets, and they come at a variety of different costs. If you are interested in utilizing a jacket for your hard cover book, ask your printer to provide you with samples from which you can choose.

Prepress
The preparation and set-up that your printer performs in order to proceed with the actual printing of the book is called prepress.

After the paper and binding method is chosen, and trim size determined, you must supply the printer with several details and electronic files in reference to your graphics (cover art) and text.

- Graphics – Graphics refer to the cover art that your designer has created for your book. Printers have specifications as to how they can receive your cover art. As different printers use different methods of printing, you must clarify with your printer the manner in which they must receive your graphics. Before your designer begins creating your cover art, know how your printer needs to receive the file, so that your designer can create the image accordingly, so as to avoid any problems that may cost you extra time and/or money to rectify.

  Malloy requires that your cover art be sent digitally, in a TIFF or EPS file, created from programs such as QuarkXPress, Adobe PageMaker, InDesign, Photoshop, Illustrator or Freehand.
- Text files – Just as for your cover art, your printer will have specifications on how your text is received. Malloy requires that your text be submitted in a PDF file, along with a printed hard copy of your text. Your qualified typesetter should be familiar with PDF files, and will probably use a program such as QuarkXPress or Adobe PageMaker to perform your text layout. Your typesetter should provide your finished text layout in the appropriate format needed by your printer.
- Colors – Most up-to-date and technologically advanced printers use the four color system – CMYK – which stands for the primary colors: cyan, magenta, yellow and also black.

  In order to create a colorful book cover, four different plates are used – one for each of the colors in the CMYK system. The cover graphics are scanned and each of the colors are separated and placed on a plate. In the printing of the cover, each plate is used, one on top of another, to create all colors.

Printers can also provide a variety of other choices for your cover, such as glossy finish, matte finish, embossing and stamping. Use other books that you like or dislike to help decide the finishing on your cover.

A qualified graphic designer will be familiar with the CMYK color separation. Again, to avoid any setbacks in time and/or cost, make it a priority to hire a qualified graphic designer that is familiar with the processes and has previous experience.

- Fonts – Your printer will also require you to submit all of the fonts used in your text as well as your cover art.
- Calculating spine bulk – When your text layout is complete and your paper thickness has been chosen, you will be able to calculate your spine bulk. Spine bulk refers to the width of your book's spine. It is important that your spine bulk is accurately calculated, as your cover designer will need to create the front cover graphics, back cover graphics and spine graphics accordingly.

  Spine bulk is especially crucial because in order for your book to maintain a professional appearance, the graphics need to be correctly placed. A miscalculation of spine bulk can result in your spine graphics bleeding into your front or back covers, creating the illusion that the cover is misaligned on the text (*please see the following page for spine bulk calculation from www.malloy.com*).

Packaging

Malloy also offers shrink wrapping services. You have the option of individually shrink wrapping each book, or shrink wrapping in bundles. Individually shrink wrapping each book will prevent your books' pages from becoming torn or dusty, however can

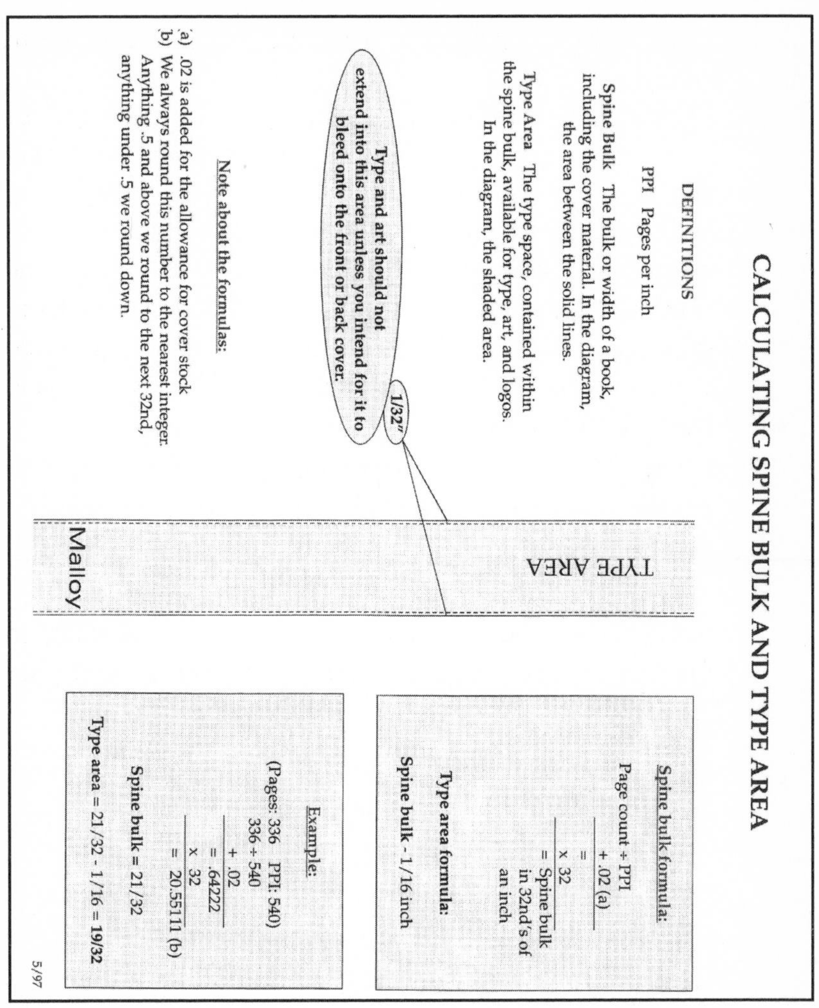

Calculating Spine Bulk

potentially prove to be disadvantageous for sales if your prospective readers are unable to peruse the contents of your book. Shrink wrapping in bundles can provide the same protection for your book as individually shrink wrapping each book, and when your book reaches its final destination, the wrap can be easily removed from the bundle and the books placed on the shelves so that readers may browse your book at their leisure.

Storage

In addition to the printing of your book, your printing company may also offer services such as inventory storage. If you find that you have no place to store your books, your printer offers inventory storage for a fee.

Fulfillment

Also, in the case that an order comes in for a large amount of books that will be extremely difficult for you to ship from your home or your small office, your printer may offer drop-shipments, wherein the printer will ship the order directly from the factory to the customer.

Copyrighting your Work

When your book is complete and arrives at your office from the printer, the first thing you should do is complete the application from the Library of Congress' Copyright Office. Filing a copyright application will protect your work and your ideas from being copied by someone else. Copyright status lasts for the entire duration of the author's life, plus 50 years after the author's death.

The process of copyrighting your work is relatively easy. You can simply visit the Library of Congress' Copyright Office Web site at http://loc.gov/copyright and complete the online application or apply via mail (*please see the following page for a sample online application and copyright page*).

Copyright Office fees are subject to change. For current fees, check the Copyright Office website at www.copyright.gov, write the Copyright Office, or call (202) 707-3000.

Form TX
For a Nondramatic Literary Work
UNITED STATES COPYRIGHT OFFICE

REGISTRATION NUMBER

TX TXU

EFFECTIVE DATE OF REGISTRATION

Month Day Year

DO NOT WRITE ABOVE THIS LINE. IF YOU NEED MORE SPACE, USE A SEPARATE CONTINUATION SHEET.

1

TITLE OF THIS WORK ▼

PREVIOUS OR ALTERNATIVE TITLES ▼

PUBLICATION AS A CONTRIBUTION If this work was published as a contribution to a periodical, serial, or collection, give information about the collective work in which the contribution appeared. Title of Collective Work ▼

If published in a periodical or serial give: Volume ▼ Number ▼ Issue Date ▼ On Pages ▼

2

a NAME OF AUTHOR ▼ — DATES OF BIRTH AND DEATH Year Born ▼ Year Died ▼

Was this contribution to the work a "work made for hire"? ☐ Yes ☐ No

AUTHOR'S NATIONALITY OR DOMICILE Name of Country OR { Citizen of ▶ / Domiciled in ▶

WAS THIS AUTHOR'S CONTRIBUTION TO THE WORK Anonymous? ☐ Yes ☐ No Pseudonymous? ☐ Yes ☐ No — If the answer to either of these questions is "Yes," see detailed instructions.

NATURE OF AUTHORSHIP Briefly describe nature of material created by this author in which copyright is claimed. ▼

b NAME OF AUTHOR ▼ — DATES OF BIRTH AND DEATH Year Born ▼ Year Died ▼

Was this contribution to the work a "work made for hire"? ☐ Yes ☐ No

AUTHOR'S NATIONALITY OR DOMICILE Name of Country OR { Citizen of ▶ / Domiciled in ▶

WAS THIS AUTHOR'S CONTRIBUTION TO THE WORK Anonymous? ☐ Yes ☐ No Pseudonymous? ☐ Yes ☐ No — If the answer to either of these questions is "Yes," see detailed instructions.

NATURE OF AUTHORSHIP Briefly describe nature of material created by this author in which copyright is claimed. ▼

c NAME OF AUTHOR ▼ — DATES OF BIRTH AND DEATH Year Born ▼ Year Died ▼

Was this contribution to the work a "work made for hire"? ☐ Yes ☐ No

AUTHOR'S NATIONALITY OR DOMICILE Name of Country OR { Citizen of ▶ / Domiciled in ▶

WAS THIS AUTHOR'S CONTRIBUTION TO THE WORK Anonymous? ☐ Yes ☐ No Pseudonymous? ☐ Yes ☐ No — If the answer to either of these questions is "Yes," see detailed instructions.

NATURE OF AUTHORSHIP Briefly describe nature of material created by this author in which copyright is claimed. ▼

NOTE

Under the law, the "author" of a "work made for hire" is generally the employer, not the employee (see instructions). For any part of this work that was "made for hire" check "Yes" in the space provided, give the employer (or other person for whom the work was prepared) as "Author" of that part, and leave the space for dates of birth and death blank.

3

a YEAR IN WHICH CREATION OF THIS WORK WAS COMPLETED — This information must be given in all cases. ◀ Year

b DATE AND NATION OF FIRST PUBLICATION OF THIS PARTICULAR WORK — Complete this information ONLY if this work has been published. Month ▶ Day ▶ Year ▶ ◀ Nation

4

COPYRIGHT CLAIMANT(S) Name and address must be given even if the claimant is the same as the author given in space 2. ▼

See instructions before completing this space.

TRANSFER If the claimant(s) named here in space 4 is (are) different from the author(s) named in space 2, give a brief statement of how the claimant(s) obtained ownership of the copyright. ▼

DO NOT WRITE HERE OFFICE USE ONLY

APPLICATION RECEIVED

ONE DEPOSIT RECEIVED

TWO DEPOSITS RECEIVED

FUNDS RECEIVED

MORE ON BACK ▶ • Complete all applicable spaces (numbers 5-9) on the reverse side of this page. • See detailed instructions. • Sign the form at line 8.

DO NOT WRITE HERE

Page 1 of ______ pages

Copyright application.

EXAMINED BY | FORM TX

CHECKED BY

☐ CORRESPONDENCE Yes

FOR COPYRIGHT OFFICE USE ONLY

DO NOT WRITE ABOVE THIS LINE. IF YOU NEED MORE SPACE, USE A SEPARATE CONTINUATION SHEET.

5

PREVIOUS REGISTRATION Has registration for this work, or for an earlier version of this work, already been made in the Copyright Office?

☐ **Yes** ☐ **No** If your answer is "Yes," why is another registration being sought? (Check appropriate box.) ▼

a. ☐ This is the first published edition of a work previously registered in unpublished form.

b. ☐ This is the first application submitted by this author as copyright claimant.

c. ☐ This is a changed version of the work, as shown by space 6 on this application.

If your answer is "Yes," give: **Previous Registration Number** ▶ **Year of Registration** ▶

6

See instructions before completing this space.

DERIVATIVE WORK OR COMPILATION

a **Preexisting Material** Identify any preexisting work or works that this work is based on or incorporates. ▼

b **Material Added to This Work** Give a brief, general statement of the material that has been added to this work and in which copyright is claimed. ▼

7

a **DEPOSIT ACCOUNT** If the registration fee is to be charged to a Deposit Account established in the Copyright Office, give name and number of Account.
Name ▼ **Account Number** ▼

b **CORRESPONDENCE** Give name and address to which correspondence about this application should be sent. Name/Address/Apt/City/State/ZIP ▼

Area code and daytime telephone number ▶ Fax number ▶

Email ▶

8

CERTIFICATION* I, the undersigned, hereby certify that I am the

Check only one ▶

☐ author
☐ other copyright claimant
☐ owner of exclusive right(s)
☐ authorized agent of ____________________

Name of author or other copyright claimant, or owner of exclusive right(s) ▲

of the work identified in this application and that the statements made by me in this application are correct to the best of my knowledge.

Typed or printed name and date ▼ If this application gives a date of publication in space 3, do not sign and submit it before that date.

Date ▶ ____________________

Handwritten signature (X) ▼

X ____

9

Certificate will be mailed in window envelope to this address:

Name ▼
Number/Street/Apt ▼
City/State/ZIP ▼

YOU MUST:
- Complete all necessary spaces
- Sign your application in space 8

SEND ALL 3 ELEMENTS IN THE SAME PACKAGE:
1. Application form
2. Nonrefundable filing fee in check or money order payable to *Register of Copyrights*
3. Deposit material

MAIL TO:
Library of Congress
Copyright Office - TX
101 Independence Avenue, S.E.
Washington, D.C. 20559-6222

Fees are subject to change. For current fees, check the Copyright Office website at www.copyright.gov, write the Copyright Office, or call (202) 707-3000.

*17 U.S.C. § 506(e): Any person who knowingly makes a false representation of a material fact in the application for copyright registration provided for by section 409, or in any written statement filed in connection with the application, shall be fined not more than $2,500.

Rev: July 2003—xxx Web Rev: July 2003 ♻ Printed on recycled paper

U.S. Government Printing Office: 2000-461-113/20,021

Copyright application.(cont.)

All rights reserved. No part of this book may be reproduced without written permission from the publisher except for the use of brief quotations in a review.

If you have purchased this book with a 'dull' or missing cover—You have possibly purchased an unauthorized or stolen book. Please immediately contact the publisher advising where, when and how you purchased this book.

Compilation and Introduction copyright © 2004 by
Triple Crown Publications
2959 Stelzer Rd., Suite C
Columbus, Ohio 43219
www.TripleCrownPublications.com

Library of Congress Control Number: 2005933943
ISBN: 0-9767894-0-X
Cover Design/Graphics: Bob James & Evangelia Philippidis, Silver Moon Graphics
Author: Vickie M. Stringer with Mia McPherson
Associate Editor: Maxine Thompson
Editor-in-Chief: Mia McPherson
Consulting: Vickie M. Stringer
Hair, Make-up and Styling: Monecka Freeman
Photography: Peter Chin

Copyright © 2005 by Triple Crown Publications. All rights reserved. No part of this book may be reproduced in any form without permission from the publisher, except by reviewer who may quote brief passages to be printed in a newspaper or magazine.
First Trade Paperback Edition Printing October 2005
10 9 8 7 6 5 4 3 2 1

Printed in the United States of America

Example of this books copyright page

The cost of the application is $30, and usually takes about 2½ 4 months to be approved and a certificate of copyright to be returned to you. The Library of Congress also requires that you mail two copies of your printed book for its archives.

Print the month and year of your anticipated copyright on the copyright page of your book. For example, if you anticipate that your book will be printed and you will submit your copyright application in January of 2010, include this on your copyright page. Your copyright page must also include your publishing company name, copyright year, ISBN and LCCN. The copyright page can also include other information such as author's name, editors' names, cover designer's name and any other information that you so choose.

Registering with Online Bookstores and Industry Web sites

Registering your book with industry Web sites is essential. In today's world, a vast number of people are computer and Internet literate, from your four-year-old nephew to your 95-year-old grandmother. Shopping online is becoming increasingly popular due to its quickness and ease.

Many readers order books online, through Web sites such as Amazon.com and bn.com (Barnes & Noble's Web site), and distributors and wholesalers become aware of new titles through a publishers' registering of a title on the company Web site.

Featuring your title on Web sites such as these gives your book national exposure in a very short amount of time. Unlike traditional bookstores, which may only appeal to a certain demographic and are limited mostly to local patrons, Web site listings allow your book to be seen nationally, by anyone at any time. Web sites don't have hours, they never close and readers don't even have to get out of bed to order.

Terms

Just like any other distributor, online bookstores have requirements that you as the publisher must meet in order to become listed on their Web sites.

- Annual Fees – many online bookstores and distributors will require the publisher to pay an annual fee in exchange for membership on their Web sites. This cost seems minimal compared to the potential exposure and sales that you will receive by listing your titles on the Web site. Depending on the pricing of your book, the annual fee could add up to a mere few sales of your book.
- Commission – Just like any other distributor, online bookstores will charge you a commission for selling your book. Many sites charge an average commission of about 55 percent, much like the 40 to 55 percent discount rate that is required by distributors.
- Agreements – Each industry Web site will have its own terms that you will be required to agree to as a member. Thoroughly review the terms before agreeing, and always keep a copy of the terms agreement in a file or folder that is easily accessible by you. Being familiar with the terms of the agreement will allow you to more effectively monitor your sales activity and gauge the success rate of utilizing the Web sites. The agreement may include several details regarding returns, pricing, additional fees, shipping and payment.

Finding the right distributor is like finding the right man. Sometimes it's a love-at-first-sight relationship. Other times, when it goes bad, it's really bad. But when you find the right distributor—the one whom you can trust to push your volumes and units and to get you everywhere—it's a dream come true.

Remember, people can't buy you if they can't find you. No amount of publishing, marketing and publicity will work without distribution. Distribution is key.

Please note: be careful of extending too

much credit. Sure you want your books out there, but if you have a distributor who won't pay you, who spends your money like it is his money, then you have a lot of inventory moved, but no sales. Set a credit limit for distributors and don't rely on their references.

After all, who gives out bad references? Judge your relationship with each distributor on an individual basis. Ask yourself: If they don't pay me, then what? I'd rather put all my money on a casino in Vegas rather than believe that all my distributors will pay.

Conquer the territory. Claim your market share. Get all over the world.

Consigners beware…

Distributors

If you want a large amount of exposure for your book and seek to sell it nationally, you will most likely need a distributor. Rather than a bookstore ordering books directly from the publishing company, it is most common for a bookstore to order its books from a distributor. Distributors act as intermediaries between stores and publishers. As a distributor has the capabilities of selling several different books from several different publishers, it is easier for stores to do one-stop shopping with a distributor rather than order from each individual publisher. Unlike wholesalers, distributors also serve to market and promote your book, and employ staff members especially to promote books to stores and get titles on the shelves.

There are many distributors from which to choose. It is important to research and choose a distributor that specializes in or is highly familiar with your genre of writing and your reading audience. Remember: a main function of a distributor is to market its books to the stores. If the distributor is unfamiliar with your subject matter, it won't be able to reach your targeted audience.

Wholesalers

Wholesalers are much like distributors in the sense that they purchase books from the publisher and sell to the stores. Where a main function of a distributor is to market books, a main function of a wholesaler is to deliver books to the stores in a fast, efficient manner. Wholesalers mainly purchase books on an as-needed basis, waiting for an order from a bookstore before ordering from the publisher instead of stocking books to market to the stores.

There are two main wholesalers in the United States: Ingram and Baker & Taylor. Both have several locations positioned in different parts of the country, allowing shipping and fulfillment times to be reduced to a minimum. Ingram's function is to sell mainly to stores, while Baker & Taylor serves other establishments such as libraries and schools.

Discounts

Each distributor and wholesaler has its own criteria for purchasing and selling a publisher's book. Research different companies' Web sites to ensure that you approach each company in the correct manner.

Once you have decided upon distributors and wholesalers, you must address the issue of discounts. Because the public buys books from the stores, the stores buy books from the distributors and the distributors buy books from you, the publisher, it is necessary for each party to buy the books at a discount from the previous party, so that everyone makes a profit. You, the publisher, sell your books to the distributor at a percentage discount. The distributor sells the books to the bookstore at a percentage discount and the bookstore sells to the reader at retail price.

The common discount that a publisher gives to a distributor is between 50 – 65 percent of your list price. This means that you will keep about 35 - 50 percent of the list price of your book, and the distributor and the bookstore divvy the remaining percentage.

Title availability

Just because a distributor or wholesaler is carrying your book does not mean that it is being made available. Check stores and other venues where your target audience should find your book. Working with a distributor or wholesaler does not mean that you can stop selling and marketing your book on your own. These companies serve to aid you in gaining exposure and making large shipments of books that you may not be able to accommodate on your own.

Payment

Getting payment from your distributors and wholesalers is likely to be the most challenging aspect of your self-publishing experience. As each distributor and wholesaler has its own terms of payment, it is extremely important to keep impeccable records and practice consistent invoicing procedures to ensure that you will get paid.

It is common for a distributor or wholesaler to have 90- to 120-day payment terms. This means that once you ship your books to the distributors or wholesalers, they have 90 to 120 days before they will remit payment to you.

It is also common for a publisher to extend an amount of credit to a distributor or wholesaler. Just as with a credit card, distributors have an allotment of credit that they can use to purchase books.

Other distributors may operate on consignment. Consignment is when a distributor does not pay the publisher until the books are sold. If the books are not sold, you are not paid.

To avoid non-payment and payment delays, some publishers may opt to demand pre-payment before books are shipped to the distributor. This is an easy way to guarantee payment, but also an easy way to cause a distributor to lose interest in carrying your book. Many distributors stick to their way of payment, and their way only.

While many distributors can be very cooperative when it comes to payment, many others are not. Below are a few important guidelines that will help to make certain that you receive payment for your books.

- Send your books and invoice for the books separately. Familiarize yourself with the different shipping and billing departments of the distribution company. If you send your invoice to the shipping address rather than the billing address, it most likely will not get to the correct people and will not be paid.
- Purchase an accounting program for your computer such as QuickBooks or Peachtree Accounting. These programs will help you to keep your shipments and your invoices organized and easy to access. These programs will also alert you when an invoice is overdue.
- Be stern and consistent with your collections procedures. If distributors notice that you are organized and consistent, they may be less likely to think that their missed payments will go unnoticed.
- Be sure that all numbers and quantities on the invoice match the numbers and quantities of the shipment and packing slip. If any number, such as purchase order number, quantity or price do not match the numbers in the distributors' database, the invoice will not be paid, and they will probably not contact you to fix the discrepancy.
- Create recourses for non-payment. Many distributors will do anything they can to avoid payment. If a distributor or wholesaler refuses to remit payment for an unreasonable

amount of time or is beyond its credit limit, stop shipping books until payment is made.

- ❖ Build relationships with your distributors. Creating positive business relations can increase accountability and trust. If you continue to be efficient, reliable and trustworthy, your distributors will enjoy working with you and may be more likely to pay you.

Returns

Another downfall to selling to a distributor or wholesaler is the returns. Imagine that you have sold 50 cases of your book to a distributor. You rush out to your local exotic car dealership, or perhaps use the money to print more books. The next month, 40 of your 50 cases of books come back to you. Returns.

Don’t assume that because your books are sold, you will receive the full amount of money for these books. Assume that at least 20 percent of your books will be returned to you. This way, you won’t overextend yourself in another area or fall into debt because your books did not sell.

Dealing with distributors and wholesalers can help you to gain the exposure necessary to successfully sell your book in stores that you would otherwise not be able to reach. However, you will take a loss, whether it is with missed payments, non-payments or returns. Be prepared for this loss, and budget accordingly.

Accounting

Keeping accurate accounts of orders, invoices and shipments is essential in collecting payment and guaranteeing long-term success for your company. Distributors have devised inventive ways to avoid and delay payment. By preparing for potential payment problems, you can counter their avoidance with your own collection solutions.

The first step in maintaining organized and precise accounts for each of your distributors is to utilize a reliable and simple accounting program. Computer programs such as Quicken, QuickBooks and Peachtree Accounting will help you to create professional invoices, keep close track of payment due dates and will alert you to past due invoices and delinquent accounts.

If you encounter a great struggle with distributors exceeding credit limits and avoiding payment, do not be afraid to take action. Stop shipments of books until the account is brought current. Provide books on a pre-pay only basis.

There are many distributors in the literary industry that are highly reliable and take pride in keeping all of their accounts current. These distributors can be a pleasure to work with. However, with the high incidence of distributor bankruptcy and delinquent accounts, these irresponsible distributors can give the rest a bad name. See Chapter 7 for more details on accounting.

6

Marketing and Advertising

I used to spend a lot of my time worrying about how to get my name out there. In fact, I found myself doing that more than working. Ironically, when I stopped worrying about how to be popular and focused more on how to work harder, I noticed that the media found me.

It's not what you say about yourself that counts. It's what others say about you. Get people talking by doing something spectacular. Be creative with your approach and use your marketing and advertising skills. You are your best sales person.

Put your best foot forward at all times. Most of all, know that if you don't believe in you, nobody else will. Do your thing.

Learn about branding and becoming a pioneer in your specialty.

Branding

While distribution may be the most challenging aspect of self-publishing, marketing is without a doubt the most important and essential aspect of your publishing company and your career as a writer. Without the proper marketing, even the greatest book ever written may never sell one copy.

Whether you brand your book, your publishing company or yourself, you must brand some aspect of your business. Your brand determines who you are; it sets you apart from the other brands or companies in your business, and helps you to stand out in a crowd.

In order to create a brand, you must know your market. By now, you should have a good deal of knowledge of the other books, authors and publishers in your genre or field. How does your company, your image, your style differ from the others? How is it similar? How do you want your work to be represented in the minds of your readers?

Once you know the answers to these questions, you are ready to create your brand. I recommend reading *The 22 Immutable Laws of Branding* by Al Ries and Laura Ries. This book will be a great tool in assisting you in creating your brand – your company name, your image and what has and hasn't worked for other brands and companies in the past. Remember: learn as much as you can from others' successes and mistakes. It will be much more economical for you in the long run.

Your brand reflects your work and your work reflects upon your brand. Readers will keep coming back to a brand—author, title, publishing company—that they trust and know to be credible. You will want to create a brand that is professional and that exudes knowledge and expertise. Your work must also reflect your brand. A reader may be drawn to an author, a title or a publishing company that appears to be credible on the surface. However, if your content doesn't support your image, don't expect that reader to come back to read your second novel, or recommend you to a friend!

Targeting your audience

One of the most important areas of marketing to a self-publisher is targeting the audience. You are an expert in your subject matter. You must also become an expert in others who are also interested in your subject matter. The concept is simple: if you've written a children's book, you want to market to children and parents. If you've written a book on surf boards, your target audience probably won't be in Alaska.

Finding your target audience

Know all of the newspapers, magazines, newsletters and events that your target audience will read and attend. Know the stores that members of your target audience will frequent. Know the Web sites and online chat forums in which members of your target audience will participate. Market, promote and sell here. You have a far better chance of selling your book to those who are already interested in your subject matter as opposed to spending the time, money and effort on trying to generate curiosity in others who know nothing of the subject or may not be interested.

Creating a Web site

Creating a Web site is a great way to bring your target audience to you. Find an experienced Web designer who can create a simple yet informational Web site about your book, your company and yourself as an author.

Providing the opportunity to purchase your book from your Web site is not only a quick, convenient way for interested persons to purchase your book, but will benefit you as the bookseller. By selling directly to the reader, you are able to keep the entire profit. Other features will also prove beneficial to sales and publicity of your company.

- ❖ Message boards—Adding a message board to your Web site is an effective way to generate interest and increase traffic on your Web site. As you bring a community of your targeted audience together, the community, as well as your sales, will grow. Discussion among your readers and prospective readers will create a buzz about your work, and your community members will be likely to recommend or discuss your book and your Web site to others in the physical community.
- ❖ Posting reviews—A Web site can also be used to post reviews of your book. Select your most favored, positive, attention-grabbing reviews to post on your Web site. The more readers are intrigued by your company and your work, the more books you will sell.
- ❖ Blurbs—The same blurbs that you will use on the cover of later editions of your book can be posted on your Web site. Put as much positive publicity on your Web site as possible. The more readers see that others have enjoyed your work, the more apt they will be to buy it themselves. When a reader sees that your book is recommended by another credible source from the literary or other enter-

tainment industries, the harder it will be for them to pass up the chance to see for themselves what all the hype is about.

- Online bookstore—Your Web site is a prime location for sales. Once your readers are hooked by the rave reviews, blurbs from credible sources and recommendations by fellow readers, your book is ready to sell itself. Have your Web designer set up an online shopping cart or create an account with PayPal or VeriSign to provide your readers and prospective customers with a safe, secure way to purchase your book. With the increasing epidemic of Internet fraud and online identity theft, readers and all other Internet shoppers are reluctant to give away any payment information to a Web site that seems unsafe. By providing a secure means of online payment, your readers will feel at ease to purchase your book and recommend it to others. See Chapter 7 for more details on secure online payment.
- Blogging—Blogs, also known as a Web logs or eJournals, have become progressively more popular and trendy on the World Wide Web. These electronic diaries can be published to your Web site on a daily or weekly basis. Effective blogs can generate high traffic to your Web site, expanding your fan and reader base. Many of the most interesting and provocative blogs have evolved into successful eBooks or traditional printed books, as they have pre-established their fan base through a Web site.
- Author bios and photos—Posting biographical information about yourself, your life and your journey as a writer and a publisher will allow readers to "get to know you" better and provide a personal connection. Knowing more about the author as a person will make your readers more likely to positively identify with you and will become

interested in seeing more of your work, traveling to a book signing or recommending you to a friend.

- Additional book information—Your Web site will give you an opportunity to refer readers to stores where your book can be found. If you choose not to accept Internet or phone orders, posting your book's availability will help to direct readers to the appropriate venue in which to find your book. Information on revised editions, upcoming events and future title releases also keep your readers interested and encourage them to become repeat customers.
- Contact information—If readers, interested distributors or other media would like to contact you, how can they do so? Include your contact information on your Web site, including phone number, fax number and e-mail address. If you'd like fan mail to be directed elsewhere than publicity inquiries, indicate to which phone number or e-mail address any questions, concerns or comments can be made, and make an effort to answer all the questions and comments you possibly can. Keeping in touch with your readers and other interested parties will help you to maintain your fan base and increase publicity and exposure.

Press Releases

Utilizing the press release is another fast, easy and relatively inexpensive way to generate publicity and reach a wide range of media and ultimately, a wide range of readers. A press release is a short, usually one-page informational piece on your book, yourself as an author or your company (*please see the following page for a sample press release from Triple Crown Publications*).

Press releases are employed by all forms of media to share and make public a piece of information. You may want to use your

FOR IMMEDIATE RELEASE

TRIPLE CROWN PUBLICATIONS releases *A Down Chick*: controversial, unadulterated novel by teen author Mallori McNeal

Columbus, OH August 26, 2005 – Triple Crown Publications, internationally renowned and pioneer hip-hop fiction publishing company, released author Mallori McNeal's first novel, *A Down Chick.* McNeal, 16, is one of the youngest authors in hip-hop lit history.

McNeal's stark and uncensored chronicle of the life of adolescent Amina Moore growing up in Cincinnati, Ohio, sparks issue and raises controversy over a young girl's exposure to abuse, neglect, sexual exploits and incarceration. Narrated in the form of a young girl's diary, Amina's daily memoirs are unanticipated and extraordinarily vivid.

McNeal began writing *A Down Chick* at the age of 14, during the summer before her first year in high school. At age 15, McNeal completed the novel and at age 16, was accepted for publication by Triple Crown Publications.

Triple Crown Publications was founded by best-selling author Vickie Stringer, after self-publishing her own provocative and controversial tale, *Let That Be the Reason.* Triple Crown Publications currently publishes over 30 novels by 20 authors.

To schedule an interview with Mallori McNeal or Vickie Stringer, please contact Triple Crown Publications at 614-478-9402.

To purchase *A Down Chick* or other Triple Crown Publications titles, contact Sales Manager Deidre Johnson at 614-478-9402 or 614-206-6587.

ISBN# 0-9762349-4-7

Contact:
Triple Crown Publications
Mia McPherson, Editor-In-Chief
614-478-9402 ext. 21
editor@triplecrownpublications.com
www.triplecrownpublications.com

Example of Press release

press release to advertise your new title, your company, your brand or your subject matter.

You will utilize your press release for marketing purposes, but the key to an effective, successful press release is to present your information in a way that it doesn't *seem* like advertisement. No prominent media outlet is going to pay attention or take seriously a press release that reads like a commercial. Successful press releases that have the potential to generate newspaper articles, magazine stories or television news stories are just that: news.

Your press release should inform the media and other literary outlets of some "breaking" aspect of your company. As an author, do you have an exceptional story? Does your book contain groundbreaking views on a controversial topic? Have you come up with a concept that is brand-new or revolutionary in your genre? Have you created a completely original genre of literature? Or, is your work simply better than everyone else's? Why? How?

Think of the successful work in the history of literature. How did J.K. Rowling's *Harry Potter* series become so wildly popular among not only children, but adults? How did Toni Morrison's *Beloved* revolutionize American literature? How did Shakespeare's work differ from the others' in his time? How did Bill Clinton's *My Life* become a best-seller?

Each of these authors and their books had a quality that set them apart from all others. What is your quality, your "IT" factor? Discover it, use it, market it. What kind of news do you like to read or hear? It is rare that you will find a news story about an average person doing average things. Capitalize on your "abnormalties" or what makes you above the average.

Once you've discovered your uniqueness, create your press

release with the complete who, what, when, where, why and how. If you don't include the complete information, your press release will appear to be unprofessional and will not be taken seriously. Whether you write your own press release or you have someone write it for you, your press release must be thoroughly edited. In literature, an author has much more freedom with language, grammar and word usage. However, your press release is expected to appear as an article in a newspaper would appear—Clear, concise, well-edited.

Send your press release to as many media and literary-industry outlets as you can find, targeting the media that will best fit your audience and your genre of work. If you've written a political book about your views on social security, you probably won't need to send a press release to *Highlights for Children* Magazine. *Newsweek* or *AARP Magazine* may be more appropriate outlets for you.

Press releases can be mailed, or more economically, e-mailed or posted to press Web sites such as www.prweb.com. In addition to including all of the who, what, when, where, why, how information, you must also create a catchy title and heading to grab the readers' attention. Imagine how many junk e-mails you get per day. Imagine how many junk e-mails an editor at *Newsweek* Magazine must get per day. You want your press release to stand out and instantly engage the reader before it ends up in the "trash" folder or the physical trash.

Also imperative to the press release is your contact name and information. You've written a catchy heading and the reader is interested in your story. How will he or she contact you? Traditionally at the very top or very bottom of your press release is where your contact information should appear.

Book Clubs/Reviewers

Research book clubs and other organizations already in existence that have reviewed books similar to yours. A simple online Google.com search such as "children's book reviewers" will point you in the right direction to where you can find Web sites, e-mail addresses and contact names to send your book for review. Once you have found these organizations, contact a staff member and inquire about the review process. Each reviewer will have its own set of rules and guidelines, so be sure to research each lead thoroughly so as to avoid wasting time and review copies of your book.

Send review copies of your book to as many credible organizations that you can find that will help you reach members of your target audience. Book clubs will often post reviews on their Web sites for others to read. The more people read your reviews and the more your book gains exposure, the more books you will sell.

Book signings and events

Researching the literary industry's events, you will find several different book signings, book expos and book conferences. Some of the major events include Book Expo America, American Library Association Book Fair, among many other national, regional and local events for literature and the arts. These events are great opportunities for networking, learning and meeting other authors and publishers.

Once your book begins to sell at the bookstores, stores may offer to host you for a book signing. Signings can be great opportunities to gain exposure and publicity through the bookstore and to sell more copies of your book, not to mention a great chance to see your fans in person, and for your fans to see you.

Whether a book store offers to host you for a book signing, or you petition a store to host you for a book signing, carefully review and research every offer. Many bookstores can make vast promises of the events that will take place, but they may not turn out as planned. Thoroughly research every event and signing before committing to attendance.

When attending a book signing, be sure that the store will have enough inventory of your title. It is also advantageous to bring something to give to your readers, such as post cards, T-shirts, bookmarks or other paraphernalia with the title, author name and company name, logo and Web address on it. Always leave the readers with something to take away with them that they can show to others.

Networking

Networking, a crucial aspect of the entire self-publishing process, is essential in marketing and publicity. Networking and getting to know other self-publishers and prominent writers, publishers and other industry people in your field will help you to learn more about your industry, keep updated on the latest developments and assist you in finding and reaching your target audience. Who better to learn from than someone who has already done so before you?

If you are writing a book on gourmet coffees, you will want to know the best coffee makers, the coffee connoisseurs, the owners of your local coffee shops, etc. Knowing the people will help you to learn the field and stay updated on all of the changes and innovations in your field. Knowing the people will help you to learn the events and gatherings that will lead to meeting more people. Knowing the owner of your local coffee shop may help you to get your gourmet coffee book into the store for sale. Through this owner, you will meet others and before you know it, your book is in all of the coffee shops, cafes and markets in the area.

On a larger scale, networking will help you gain broader exposure citywide, statewide, nationwide and worldwide. The more people who know you will know your book. The more people that know about your book will buy your book.

Using your Product to Market Itself

You will be spending money to have your book produced and printed anyway, so why not use your book to advertise itself?

Cover art

Your book's cover art is often the first thing noticed about your book. Even if a reader has never heard of or seen your book before, effective and attractive cover art can entice and generate intrigue. Choose a cover design that represents your book, your content and yourself well. Professionalism is key. Think of the types of covers you have seen on other books. Which ones were effective? Which were not effective?

Author name

How many times have you read a book simply because of the author's name? If you have read a great book by an author, you will likely purchase another book by the same author. By the same token, if you've heard great or intriguing things about a certain author, you may be likely to purchase a book by that author, even if you know little about the content of the book. Your author name is part of your image and ultimately part of your brand. You will want to build name recognition.

Order form

Including an order form in the back of your book is an extremely effective way to generate additional sales. If a reader has enjoyed a book that he or she has just read, that reader wants to know how to purchase more books like it. If you publish more than one title, you can use each title to promote the others. If you have published one title, you can use that copy of the title to generate more sales of the same book. Often times, readers borrow books from others or from the library. If the reader desires to purchase one of the books for his or her own use or for a friend, what simpler way to do so than with an order form that is already in his or her hands? The reader needs not search the Web or look elsewhere to buy (*please see the following page for a sample back-of-book order form from Triple Crown Publications*).

Blurbs

Including blurbs from other authors, publishers or prominent people in literature or in your genre of writing adds credibility to your work. If someone important thinks highly of your work, readers will be more inclined to think that they, too, will enjoy your work. For the same reasons that fast food restaurants and athletic shoe companies use celebrities to market their products, you are using the words of prominent figures to sell your book. If someone you admire says that he or she likes something, you'll be curious to try it as well.

Synopsis

An intriguing, thought provoking synopsis is also a helpful tool in marketing your book. When in a bookstore, readers often look to the synopsis on the back cover of a book to determine whether or not they will be interested in the book's content. Spend time creating an effective, illustrative and descriptive synopsis – but not *too* descriptive. Give readers just enough detail to entice them to

ORDER FORM

Triple Crown Publications
2959 Stelzer Rd.
Columbus, Oh 43219

Name: ______________________

Address: ______________________

City/State: ______________________

Zip: ______________________

	TITLES	PRICES
	Dime Piece	$15.00
	Gangsta	$15.00
	Let That Be The Reason	$15.00
	A Hustler's Wife	$15.00
	The Game	$15.00
	Black	$15.00
	Dollar Bill	$15.00
	A Project Chick	$15.00
	Road Dawgz	$15.00
	Blinded	$15.00
	Diva	$15.00
	Sheisty	$15.00
	Grimey	$15.00
	Me & My Boyfriend	$15.00
	Larceny	$15.00
	Rage Times Fury	$15.00
	A Hood Legend	$15.00
	Flipside of The Game	$15.00
	Menage's Way	$15.00

SHIPPING/HANDLING (Via U.S. Media Mail) **$3.95**

TOTAL **$**__________

FORMS OF ACCEPTED PAYMENTS:

Postage Stamps, Institutional Checks & Money Orders, all mail in orders take 5-7 Business days to be delivered.

Example of back of book Order Form

read further. Don't give away too much; otherwise there will be no purpose in reading the entire book.

Bar code, ISBN and retail price

Even with the best marketing and publicity on the planet, your book will be nothing without the proper displayed information. *Always* include a Bar code on the back of your book, which will display your ISBN and the retail price of your book. If your book is missing any of these three items, it is likely that a distributor, wholesaler, store or reader will reject your book. Would you spend your hard-earned money on anything that didn't have the proper notations clearly displayed? When you can't find a price on an item, are you likely to buy it? If you are a bookstore owner and you can't clearly display the cost of the book to your customers, what are the chances that you will risk carrying a book that readers won't buy? The answer is very slim, if any chance at all. Do not forget your Bar code, ISBN or retail price on your book!

Paid Advertisements

Paid advertisements, such as those in magazines and trade publications should be used only when all other free and creative means of advertising and publicity have been exhausted. Paid advertisements are not only costly, but ineffective when the proper foundation is not in place.

Paid advertisements can be effective when you have already generated a strong reader-base and are looking to expand. Paid advertisements help to maintain popularity and broaden your scope, but should not be used with the intentions of generating the initial interest. Let your news stories, events, book signings, Web site and other free publicity provoke the interest of readers. Use paid advertisements to maintain your presence.

Your Purpose for Writing and Selling

When marketing and selling your book, it is important to keep in perspective why you have written the book, and why you want to sell it.

Of course, you want to make money. But, is that what initially inspired you to write in the first place? In order to be able to successfully market your book, the answer should be no. Did you write a book about your own experiences to help inspire others? Do you have a certain expertise that you want to share with the world?

The purpose of writing and publishing should be for the sake of sharing and spreading your vision and knowledge to others. Your vision and knowledge makes you unique from all others. Expand on your uniqueness and your "IT" factor and others will be eager to share and take part in your vision.

7

Fulfillment

When I first thought about fulfillment and producing, I was not prepared for the volume of success that I received. So when it comes down to fulfillment, be prepared for your demand. I used to run out of packing tape, boxes, everything—you name it.

When I couldn't afford boxes, I found out about stores which gave out free boxes from their own shipments, and on what days. When your customers say they want their book, be certain to get it to them as soon as possible.

Let's find out how.

Storing your Inventory

Whether you are shipping your books out of your home, office or storage facility, you must secure a climate-controlled area for the storage of your books. Your books are now your livelihood—any damage to your books will mean damage to your product, your sales and your company.

If you plan to store your books in your home, secure a cool, dry room with a sturdy floor. For the sake of shipping and fulfillment of orders, it will be easiest to store books on your first floor, as it will be much easier to carry or transport books from the first floor to your car or carrier truck, rather than walking them up and down stairs several times.

Storing your books in a garage can also be useful in easy transportation, however the garage must be dry and support proper air circulation. In many instances, book pages can become warped, damaged or discolored if stored in a damp, stale environment.

No matter where you choose to store your books, it is suggested that you keep the books in the original packaging in which you received them from the printer. If you have to remove books from the packaging, keep the remainder of the unused books in boxes. Exposed books can result in the dulling of the colors on your book cover, wear and tear and discolored pages. The less your books are handled, the better condition in which they will remain. Here are a few tips for proper storage of your books:

1. When storing books, avoid stacking any box of books directly on the floor. Keep the first book of your stack elevated at least a few inches off of the floor, and away from the wall. This will allow for proper air circulation, and prevent your product from quick deterioration. This will

also help to prevent damage from any water or other liquid spills, flooding or leakage.

2. When stacking boxes, keep the stacks short enough so that you may easily reach the top box and avoid the risk of toppling boxes. Damaged books mean decreased sales and profit loss. The best you can do with a damaged book is to sell it at a deep discount or donate it to a local library or other institution.
3. Only order what you have enough room to store. Large orders can be shipped directly from a printer that offers drop-shipment services, but also be sure to keep enough inventory for sending review copies and fulfilling mail, phone or Web-generated orders.

Shipping to individuals

Shipping directly to the reader is one of the best ways that a publisher can receive payment. Often with orders shipped directly to the reader, you as the publisher will receive the full retail price of the book, plus a reasonable amount for shipping and handling costs.

There are three common methods of shipping directly to the reader – mail order, phone order and Web order. No matter what method you choose to utilize, make your shipping procedures well known to your customers. Clearly post your shipping policies, return policies and turn-around times on your Web site and order forms. Your readers will be eager to have your book in their hands the instant they place their orders, and will need to be clear on the amount of time that it will take you to process and ship the orders.

Mail order

You as the publisher may or may not choose to accept orders

through the mail. While it is common to extend credit to a wholesaler, distributor or reputable bookstore, it is not common to extend credit to individuals. In order for an individual to receive a book through mail order, you should request payment upfront, before shipping your book to the reader. Payment can be taken a number of different ways, most commonly through personal checks or money orders. Direct your orders to be sent to your P.O. Box address. This will help you to keep all orders organized and in one location.

As some publishers have encountered difficulty with bad or bouncing checks, some have shied away from accepting mail order payment. Waiting for a check to clear through your bank before shipping an order can become a lengthy process. You must keep close account of whom the check came from, the corresponding order and the prompt shipment of the order once the check clears.

Keep a log book or electronic file of all orders that you receive, the type of payment that is used and the date of shipment. This will be very useful in the event that a customer calls to inquire about the status of his or her order.

Phone order

You may or may not choose to utilize phone orders as another form of individual sale. Phone orders are convenient for those readers who do not have access to a computer or the Internet, those who are wary of giving away personal or credit card information online or those who prefer the ease of a phone call to place an order as opposed to waiting for the United States Postal Service to deliver a check or money order to you.

Phone orders will require you to be able to process credit card information, over the phone, at your office. To do this, you will need to acquire merchant status. Research banks that provide merchant status to business owners. Different banks employ different policies and fees, and some may be wary of granting merchant status with the high incidence of phone and Internet order fraud. Although you can apply for merchant status through private agencies, banks are the safest institutions through which to operate.

In order to process credit card orders over the phone, you will need equipment—either a mini-terminal similar to credit card machines used at most retail stores or a software program such as PC Authorize or MAC Authorize. The credit card companies will charge a small fee per each transaction or sale, and your bank may charge you fees associated with becoming a merchant.

The process of gaining merchant status and obtaining a credit card machine can become lengthy, and costs are involved. If you find that you receive several phone order requests –enough for you to want to incur the costs of merchant status and credit card machines—this may be a good venture for you.

It can also be simple to refer your phone customers to your Web site for ordering by credit card, or if you accept mail orders, to send a check or money order for their purchases.

Web order

A great many of your sales will also come from your effectively-promoted and professional Web site. Web orders are fast and easy. Once your prospective reader becomes interested in your work and visits your Web site – complete with rave reviews from book clubs and reviewers, and blurbs from the important people in your industry – the sale will come easily.

Display the link to your electronic order form clearly enough for your reader to see it without much searching. Your Web designer will be able to help you to create a secure site for ordering. With the rising incidence of identity theft and Internet fraud, online buyers have become wary of giving up valuable personal and credit card information to sites that seem unsecure. Have your Web designer set you up with a secure shopping cart or create an account through online payment providers such as PayPal or VeriSign.

Companies such as PayPal and VeriSign are set up to accept most forms of payment through the Internet. They allow your company to accept all major credit cards, debit cards and most checks, and allow you and your customers the security of a safe system through which to make transactions. They also provide services such as online sales reports and automatic calculation of shipping fees and applicable taxes. Most often, there are no monthly or annual fees involved, however a fee is charged on each transaction made through the provider. For more information, visit www.paypal.com or www.verisign.com.

Generating individual sales

Individual sales can be effectively generated in many ways. As stated in the marketing and publicity chapter, you must use both conventional and creative ways to generate sales, and be sure to track the success of each of the methods that you use.

One of the most common ways to generate individual sales is through your order form. You can have your graphic designer assist you in generating an eye-catching order form that you can use to mail to prospective readers.

Another useful way to utilize your order form is to place one in the back of every book that you publish. If you publish more than one title, you can use each title to advertise the others. If you've published one title, readers who have borrowed the book from a friend, a library or who wish to order another copy for themselves or for others can do so with ease.

It will be very easy for you to track the sales generated from the back-of-the-book order form, as you will be able to identify the torn-out sheet of paper easily. You will likely find that the majority of your individual orders will be generated by this order form.

Make sure that you include the price of the book, along with any tax or shipping charges, and the address, phone number and/or Web site where your reader can mail or electronically send his or her order form and payment.

Is your order missing something?

If you happen to receive an individual order that is missing something – and you will, whether it is an order form without payment or payment without specification of order – you will need to correspond with the reader in order to fulfill his or her request. Create a form letter on your company letterhead, specifying the additional information that is needed to complete the reader's order. To save yourself postage, ask for readers' e-mail addresses and phone numbers on your order form. If you do not receive response via e-mail or phone, it will still be necessary to mail a form letter (*please see the following pages for sample letters from Triple Crown Publications*).

Be polite and cordial to your readers. More often than not, your reader misunderstood the terms of sale and will be cooperative and quick in returning the necessary payment or order information to you. A happy, satisfied reader is more likely to be a returning customer or refer your titles to a friend.

Triple Crown Publications

2959 Stelzer Rd.
Suite C
Columbus, OH 43219

614.478.9402
614.478.9403

Date

Name
Address
City, State, Zip

Dear (Reader),

We received the money order that you sent for (amount). We thank you for your order.

However, you did not indicate which books you would like to receive. Enclosed is an order form that you may use to indicate which books you would like to receive. Please also include the address that you would like the books mailed to.

Please return this order form back to us so that we may complete your order.

Thank you for supporting Triple Crown Publications!

Sincerely,

Triple Crown Publications
Shipping Department

Empowering Writers and Enlightening Minds
www.triplecrownpublications.com

Sample letter of Money with no Order

Triple Crown Publications

2959 Stelzer Rd.
Suite C
Columbus, OH 43219

614.478.9402
614.478.9403

Date

Name
Address
City, State, Zip

Dear (Reader):

We recently received your order for 2 Triple Crown titles. We thank you for your order.

However, before we can ship your books, we must receive payment with your order form. Enclosed is your original order form. Please return the form with your payment so that we may proceed with your shipment.

Thank you for supporting Triple Crown Publications!

Sincerely,

Triple Crown Publications
Shipping Department

Empowering Writers and Enlightening Minds
www.triplecrownpublications.com

Sample letter of Order with no Money

Shipping to Distributors, Wholesalers, Stores and Libraries

Shipments to distributors, wholesalers, stores and libraries will be on a much larger scale than individuals' orders.

For orders that are too large to ship from your personal inventory, a printer that provides drop-shipment services can handle this fulfillment.

For large orders that you will fulfill out of your own inventory, you will need to utilize a large parcel shipping service such as UPS, FedEx, DHL or other. By using one of these carriers, you have the ability to track shipments and ensure customers' receipt of their orders in a timely manner. Work to establish relationships with your local mail carriers and delivery people. This will enable you to secure set pick-up and delivery times, and help you to be prepared to ship your daily orders in a timely manner.

When packaging large orders, it may be possible to keep cases in the same packaging in which they arrived to you from your printer, and affix a separate label with the necessary shipping information. Most carriers have programs that you can download on your computer or online shipping services that make it simple to input your return address, customers' shipping addresses, customers' phone numbers and weight of package so that you can print a shipping label from your desktop.

Scales can be purchased in order to calculate the exact postage for large and small shipments. Using a scale will ensure that you are paying sufficient postage for your order to be sent and received in a timely manner, and will also prevent you from spending extra money by over-estimating package weights.

A postage meter is also helpful in shipping smaller packages and envelopes via USPS. While stamps always work, metered postage offers a professional, polished look to your package and can be faster and more efficient than peeling and sticking multiple stamps to an envelope or package. Postage meter machines can be ordered through companies such as Pitney Bowes, which charge monthly or annual fees for the postage and also the rental of the machine.

Envelopes and packaging are important in maintaining your company's professional image. Often times, mail carriers will provide free packaging to ship with their services. Utilize as much free packaging as possible.

Back orders, Reprints, Revisions

If you run out of your product, don't make your customers wait too long to hear the news or to receive their order. Create a form letter or post card stating which titles are on back order, which are in reprint, which may be out of print or in revision. Inform your customers that their business is very important to you and appreciated, and provide them with a date that they can expect to receive their order (*please see the following page for a sample "out of stock" card from Triple Crown Publications*).

Some customers will be sympathetic, while some will not. You must be prepared to replace a customer's order with a different title or refund his or her money.

Order Processing

Once you have received an order, it is extremely important that you process the order in an organized, efficient and carefully doc-

Triple Crown Publications
P.O. BOX 7212
Columbus, OH 43205

Out Of The Following Titles:

- [ ] The Game
- [ ] Let That Be The Reason
- [ ] Gangsta
- [ ] A Hustler's Wife
- [ ] Dollar Bill
- [ ] Imagine This
- [ ] A Project Chick
- [ ] Black

Your Order Was Shipped As Of:

____

Comments

____

____

____

Dear Faithful Customer,

We are very disappointed to tell you that the title that you recently ordered from Triple Crown Publications is currently out of stock. A re-order has been made and when they arrive your titles will be shipped first to assure that you get them within a respectable time frame. For additional information, see details to your left on current titles out of stock and when the ship date will be. If you have any more questions, feel free to visit us on the web at www.triplecrownpublications.com.

Thank you for your patience,

Triple Crown Publications
Ordering Center

Sample "out of stock" card

umented manner. Computer accounting programs such as QuickBooks and Peachtree Accounting allow you to easily process, document and track all of your shipments, invoices and packaging slips and will alert you when payments are due.

When shipping an order, your program will allow you to print three copies of each processed order.

- Packing slip—The first copy, the packing slip, will detail the customer's purchase order or invoice number, customer's shipping information, your mailing information and the quantities of goods shipped, but not the price of each item nor the total amount due. You will affix the packing slip on one or more of the boxes or envelopes that you ship to your customer using an adhesive, clear sleeve that will be supplied by your carrier. The customer's shipping information, purchase order number or invoice number should be clearly visible. The packing slip allows your customer's receiving department to be clear on the contents of the package.
- Invoice—The second copy, the invoice copy, will detail the customer's purchase order number, invoice number, shipping and billing information, quantities of goods shipped, price of each quantity, total amount due and payment terms/due date. Also included on the invoice will be the percentage discount received, and the method of shipment and tracking information. Invoices can be mailed at any time you choose, but it is efficient to mail your invoice on the same day as you ship the corresponding order. Know the correct person, department and billing address of your customer. You should clarify this information upon agreement to payment terms or when you receive the customer's order.

Sending an invoice to the correct person, department and billing address is imperative. Many times, distributors, wholesalers and stores will do anything they can to avoid or delay payment to you. You want to give them as few opportunities as possible to succeed in this.

- Your record—The third copy is for your records. This copy is an exact duplicate of the invoice. Always keep accurate accounts of all orders shipped. Create separate files for each of your customers, detailing the agreed-upon terms, discounts and contact names, phone and fax numbers, e-mail and mailing addresses of important people in shipping, purchasing and accounting departments. You will need to refer to these records several times when you are collecting payment.

Receiving payment

Even if you've gotten all of your invoicing right, sent the invoice to your customer to the correct person at the correct billing address, the accounts payable office is able to successfully match the invoice with the package received, everything arrived in a timely manner, etc., you may still encounter a struggle for your payment.

As mentioned in Chapter 5, each company has its own terms. Many times, when payment time rolls around, companies will attempt to avoid payment or delay payment with several different tactics, including returns or demanding P.O.D.—proof of delivery.

- Returns—As payment time nears, you may find that you receive a good percentage of the books that you sent out in returns. It is common for a publisher to receive 10 to 30 percent of the total books shipped in returns. Read the terms of agreement for each distributor, wholesaler or store carefully, so that you are familiar with the returns policy. At the end of a customer's 90- to 120-day pay cycle, you may be expecting a significant check for the orders that you shipped. Instead, you may receive many returns, and a significantly smaller check than what you had expected.

If your customers have not sold all of the books ordered from you, they will attempt to deplete the remaining inventory and lower the cost of the bill owed to you. As stated in Chapter 5, **expect to receive returns**. Don't count on receiving the total amount owed to you, and always budget assuming that you will receive returns.

- P.O.D.—When your customer asks you to provide P.O.D., your carrier tracking information comes handy, which you can often access online and usually requires a signature from the recipient. Take your copy of the invoice from your files and send a copy of this along with the tracking information to your customer. Remember to keep all copies of tracking information, invoices and record the date and time that you sent each P.O.D., as you may be asked to supply this information more than once.

The more information you have and the more organized you are with your shipments and invoices, the less likely your customers will be able to avoid payment or label you as an easy target.

8

So Now Your Book is a Success

Enjoy! Pop the top on that bubbly and sit back. Job well done! However, with success come great pitfalls. Now the lawsuits. Now the issues. And sometimes, even ungratefulness from those who you helped.

But remember, you've earned this rise to fame. Claim it and now prepare to have a consistent presence in the marketplace. Study incessantly to increase your skills and your marketability. Learn to sustain your success as well as to achieve it. Make your success lucrative and meaningful for you.

In the end, publishing a book is still a business and you can't be afraid to admit this.

Congratulations! Your book is now a complete success. You are selling so many books, you are having trouble keeping up with the demand. You are outgrowing your home office and your garage is at full capacity with books. You've gotten so many orders that you have hired a shipping clerk and an assistant to help you with organizing files, paperwork and accounting. You're becoming overwhelmed with fan mail. Your success as a self-publisher has exceeded even your wildest dreams.

The problem? You don't know what to do now. Should you expand your home office into a new office space? Should you invest your earnings into hiring more staff in the hopes of generating even more business? Should you write another book? Should you publish someone else's book?

You have several options. Many successful self-publishers go on to negotiate book deals with a larger publishing company. Others choose to expand their own company to include more titles by other authors, or write additional books themselves. Still others can do all of the above, and delve into agenting. The facets of the publishing industry are countless, and you are only limited by your imagination!

The Majors Will Now Come Calling

Now that your book has become increasingly popular, the major publishers – who not long ago rejected your work—will come calling with a book deal.

If you find that your book is selling so fast that you are having trouble keeping up with demand, you've grown increasingly frustrated with the empty promises of payment from your distributors and your house has become inundated with mail, boxes and paperwork, negotiating a book deal with a major publisher could be worth consideration. It will be an opportunity for you to expand your readership and reach outlets that you could not with your small company.

Because your self-published book has shown a good sales record and you have developed your reader base, your work is now more appealing to the large publishing companies. As you've already begun to carve out your own niche in the literary industry, a larger publisher will see your work as a greater profit for less effort. You've already done the footwork and laid the foundation. A larger publisher will still work to promote your book and increase its popularity and sales, but will find much more ease in doing so because you've already jump-started the publicity and marketing process.

On the fateful day that the major publisher contacts you, be prepared. There are many components of the negotiation process of which you will need to be well-informed in order to achieve the best deal for you and your work.

Contracts

The first thing that you must be familiar with is the contract. The contract will most likely be lengthy, and contain several clauses littered with legal jargon that may be difficult to comprehend. If a major publishing company approaches you with a contract, seek legal advice. You must read and comprehend every clause in the contract. Do not be distracted by large advances. Before signing anything, you should fully comprehend your rights and the terms of the agreement. This agreement will determine your fate and the fate of your work. This merits much deliberation and consideration on your part.

Advances

Advances are the sums of money that a publisher will pay to an author in advance of the actual sales of the book. Advances are not free money. Any advance amount that you are paid will come out of your future royalties. In other words, if a publisher pays you $5,000 in advance payments, you will have to wait until your book sells over $5,000 in royalties before you see another dime. Now, imagine this amount on a much larger scale. How long will it be before your book has earned back the amount of the advances? It could take months or years. Some book sales never exceed the amount in advances. This means that after your advance payments, it could be a very long time, if ever, that you see any profits from your book.

Advances are normally broken down into a series of smaller payments. Different publishers operate on different terms. Be aware of when your advance payments are due.

Royalties

Royalties are the percentage of book sales that actually go to you. On average, an author's royalty rates are around 5 to 10 percent of the book's sales. Depending on the terms of your contract, this could be 5 to 10 percent of the retail value of the book, or of the actual sale value. There are huge differences in these two figures. Ten percent of the retail value of a $20.00 novel amounts to much more than 10 percent of the actual sale value of the same novel. If the novel is discounted at a bookstore for half price, your royalty rate will be 10 percent of $10.00.

Royalties are paid on a different schedule as advance payments. Where advances are usually paid within a few weeks or months of each other, royalties are often paid quarterly or semi-annually. Royalties are not like paychecks that come every two weeks. It's more like every 6 months.

Growing Your Small Company

Now that your first self-published book is a success, your readers will want more. You can choose to expand your library of titles by writing another one yourself, or you may choose to publish other authors' work.

Writing another book

As you are well aware, writing a book takes time. If you choose to author another book yourself, you will need to put the necessary time, effort and attention into your writing. However, you can't neglect the needs of your publishing company. If you choose to write another book, you may begin to look into hiring additional staff to ease some of the workload of running your publishing company. You have worked long and hard to make your book a success. When hiring staff, make sure that you choose the most qualified and dependable candidates. Continue to promote your first book while you also begin to promote the upcoming sequel or second work.

Signing new authors

Along your writing and publishing journey, through networking and meeting with others in the literary community, you may have come upon other talented writers who you feel will be very successful and marketable in the right hands.

When signing another author, you will have to create a contract complete with advances and royalty rates. Consult with your lawyer when creating a contract so as to protect yourself as the publisher and your author from potential legal issues.

If you haven't yet discovered your next best-selling author but hope to do so, or you have met others who claim to have written the next best-seller, you will need to create guidelines in which you would like to have work submitted to you and reviewed. Include a copy of your submission guidelines on your Web site and refer interested parties to the guidelines frequently. Sticking closely to your guidelines will keep the selection process organized, efficient and fair to all.

Assisting newcomers

When you have arrived as a successful author and publisher, you will find that many people want to know your secret; how you did it. You were there once, too, remember? You networked to learn how to start you company, to learn who the great Web designers were and how to become involved in the industry events. It is up to you whether and how much you choose to assist others in their quest to self-publish. Don't forget how grateful you were when someone important graced you with a few pearls of wisdom!

Agenting

You've made your book a success. You've published other authors and made their books successes, too. You find that so many people are looking to you for guidance and assistance and are asking you how to choose the next best-seller. Why not make money doing it?

Once you've proved your knack for picking a great manuscript, producing and marketing a successful and highly sought-after product, others will ask you to do the same for them. Agenting may be a lucrative avenue for you!

By becoming an agent, you are essentially selling an author's manuscript to another publishing company—usually one of the majors. Because of your proven winning track record, the editors at the large publishing companies will value your opinion, and will be likely to purchase a novel that is recommended by you.

As an author's agent, when the large publishing company decides to offer your author a book deal, you are entitled to a percentage of the royalties. You did much of the leg-work, now you can sit back and enjoy some of the profits.

You thought that turning your book into a best-seller would be the end of the road, when in fact, it is just the beginning. Now that you have the literary world at your fingertips, what will your next step be?

Index

A

B

C

Index

Index

Index

Resources

This is a list of recommended business and individuals with whom I have had exceptional experiences. Before utilizing services from any business or individual, thoroughly and diligently research each lead.

Agents

The Vines Agency
Contact: James C. Vines
648 Broadway Suite 901
New York, New York 10012
212-777-5522 phone
212-777-5978 fax
JV@vinesagency.com
www.vinesagency.com

Triple Crown Management
2959 Stelzer Road Suite C
Columbus, Ohio 43219
614-478-9402 phone
614-478-9403 fax
www.triplecrownpublications.com

Resources

Bar Codes

Film Masters
11680 Hawke Road
Columbia Station, Ohio 44028
(440) 748-8060 phone
(440) 748-2258 fax
www.filmmasters.com

R.R. Bowker/U.S. ISBN Agency
630 Central Avenue
New Providence, New Jersey 07974
1-877-310-7333 phone
908-219-0188 fax
isbn-san@bowker.com
www.isbn.org

Copyright

Copyright Office
Library of Congress
101 Independence Avenue SE
Washington, DC 20559
202-707-3000 phone
www.loc.gov/copyright
www.copyright.gov

Distributors/Wholesalers

Afrikan World Books
Contact: Nati Kamau-Nataki
2217 Pennsylvania Avenue
Baltimore, Maryland 21217
410-383-2006 phone
410-383-0511 fax
afrikanworldword@aol.com
www.afrikanworldbooks.com

Ingram Book Group
Contact: Pam Tucker
14 Ingram Boulevard
LaVergne, Tennessee 37086
615-213-5544 phone
615-213-5428 fax
pam.tucker@ingrambook.com

Inner City Business Ventures, Inc.
Contact: Bob Romanow
330 Martin Luther King Boulevard
Roxbury, Massachusetts 02119
617-541-0197 phone
617-541-0285 fax

Resources

Editorial Services

Black Butterfly Press
Contact: Dr. Maxine Thompson
P.O. Box 5655
Inglewood, California 90310-5655
323-242-9917 phone
323-242-9819 fax
MaxTho@aol.com
www.sucess-talk.com
www.voiceamerica.com
www.artistfirst.com
www.maxineshow.com

Chloe Hilliard
chloehilliard@aol.com

Mia McPherson
miamcpherson@yahoo.com

Graphic Services

Marion Designs
Contact: Keith Saunders
225 Sunderland Way Suite #B
Stockbridge, Georgia 30281
678-641-8689 phone
mariondesigns@bellsouth.net
www.MarionDesigns.com

Silver Moon Graphics
Contact: Bob James & Evangelia Philippidis
www.silvermoon-graphics.com
athena1157@aol.com

ISBN

R.R. Bowker/US ISBN Agency
630 Central Avenue
New Providence, New Jersey 07974
1-877-310-7333 phone
908-219-0188 fax
isbn-san@bowker.com
www.isbn.org

LCCN

The Library of Congress
101 Independence Avenue SE
Washington, DC 20540
202-707-5000 - phone
www.lcweb.loc.gov

Legal Expertise/Literary Law

F. Robert Stein
Pryor Cashman Sherman Flynn
410 Park Avenue

New York, NY 10022
212 326 0830 - phone
212 798 6914 - fax
rstein@pryorcashman.com
www.pryorcashman.com
Rate: $435.00 per hour

Printing

Malloy Inc.
Tim Scarbrough, Sales
5411 Jackson Road
Ann Arbor, Michigan 48106
800-722-3231 extension 502
734-913-8566 fax
www.malloy.com
tim_scarbrough@malloy.com

Print on Demand Publishers

Author House
1663 Liberty Drive
Suite 200,
Bloomington IN 47403
www.authorhouse.com
(888)519-5121

Resources

Shipping Services

UPS: www.ups.com

FedEx: www.fedex.com

DHL: www.dhl.com

USF: www.usfc.com

United States Postal Service: www.usps.gov

Typesetting Services

Holscher Type and Design
242 W. North Street
Waynesboro, PA 17268
(717) 762-4666 phone
holsch@comcast.net

Reference & Recommended Readings

The Self-Publishing Manual by Dan Poynter. Para Publishing, 2003.

The 22 Immutable Laws of Branding by Al Ries and Laura Ries. CollinsBusiness, 2002.

The Complete Guide to Self-Publishing by Tom & Marilyn Ross. Writer's Digest Books, 2002.

How to Start and Run a Small Book Publishing Company by Peter I. Hupalo. HCM Publishing, 2002.

Editing Fact and Fiction, A Concise Guide to Book Editing by Leslie T. Sharpe and Irene Gunther. Cambridge University Press, 1994.

ePublishing for Dummies by Victoria Rosenborg. IDG Books Worldwide, Inc., 2001.

The Associated Press Stylebook and Briefing on Media Law by Associated Press. Perseus Publishing, 2002.

The MLA Style Manual and Guide to Scholarly Publishing 2d ed by Joseph Gibaldi. Modern Language Association of America, 1998.